SAMS TEACH YOURSELF PALMPILOT™ AND PALM III™ IN 10 MINUTES

Michael Steinberg

in 10 Minutes

SAMS

A Division of Macmillan Computer Publishing
201 West 103rd St., Indianapolis, Indiana, 46290 USA

Copyright© 1999 by Sams Publishing

FIRST EDITION
FIRST PRINTING—1999

All rights reserved. No part of this book shall be reproduced, stored in a retrieval system or transmitted by any means, electronic, mechanical, photocopying, recording, or otherwise, without permission from the publisher. No patent liability is assumed with respect to the use of the information contained herein. Although every precaution has been taken in the preparation of this book, the publisher and author assume no responsibility for errors or omissions. Neither is any liability assumed for damages resulting from the use of the information contained herein. For information, address Sams Publishing, 201 W. 103rd St., Indianapolis, IN 46290.

International Standard Book Number: 0-672-31452-5

Library of Congress Catalog Card Number: 98-86978

01	00	99		4	3	2	1

Interpretation of the printing code: the rightmost double-digit number is the year of the book's printing; the rightmost single-digit, the number of the book's printing. For example, a printing code of 99-1 shows that the first printing of the book occurred in 1999.

Composed in AGaramond by Macmillan Computer Publishing

Printed in the United States of America

EXECUTIVE EDITOR
Jim Minatel

ACQUISITIONS EDITOR
Renee Wilmeth

MANAGING EDITOR
Thomas F. Hayes

COPY EDITOR
Keith Cline

INDEXER
Angie Bess

PRODUCTION
Laura Knox
Louis Porter, Jr.
Daniela Raderstorf

PROOFREADER
Lynne J. Miles-Morillo

OVERVIEW

Introduction

1	Getting to Know Your Palm Organizer
2	More Hardware Operations
3	Maneuvering the Main Display
4	Manual Data Entry
5	Maximizing Your Palm–Preferences and Applications
6	Applications–Address Book
7	Applications–Date Book
8	Applications–To Do List
9	Applications–Memo Pad
10	Applications–Expense
11	Applications–Calculator
12	Applications–Mail
13	Applications–Security
14	Additional Palm Programs and Utilities
15	Initial PC Hardware and Software Setup
16	Desktop Software–Address Book
17	Desktop Software–Date Book
18	Desktop Software–To Do List
19	Desktop Software–Memo Pad
20	How to HotSync
21	Adding a New Application to Your Palm
A	A List of Suggested Web Sites

Contents

Introduction xiii

1 Getting to Know Your Palm Organizer   1
Choosing a Palm Computer 2
Quick Tour 4
Starting Up 5
Displaying the Backlight 7
Adjusting the Contrast 7

2 More Hardware Operations   9
Removing the Stylus..9
Changing the Batteries in Your Palm Computer.........................10
Resetting the System...12
Adding Memory 16

3 Maneuvering the Main Display   17
Touring the Main Display...17
Soft Buttons 18

4 Manual Data Entry   27
Entering Data with Graffiti 27
Entering Data with the Onscreen Keyboard 31

5 Maximizing Your Palm—Preferences and Applications   38
Preferences 38
Getting to the Preferences Menu 39
Palm Applications, Preferences, General 40
Palm Applications, Preferences, Buttons 45
Palm Applications, Preferences, Digitizer 52

Palm Applications, Preferences, Formats 53
Palm Applications, Preferences, Modem 55
Palm Applications, Preferences, Network 58
Palm Applications, Preferences, Owner 62
Palm Applications, Preferences, ShortCuts 63
Using ShortCuts 66

6 Applications—Address Book   68

Using the Address Book 68
Using Categories 73
Menu Commands 78

7 Applications—Date Book   82

Date Book 82
Adding a New Entry 85
Viewing Event Details 86
Additional Viewing Options 90
Menu Commands 92
Menu Commands—Options 93

8 Applications—To Do List   98

To Do List 98
Menu Commands 104

9 Applications—Memo Pad   108

Using the Memo Pad 108
Private 115
Menu Commands—Options 116

10 Applications—Expense   118

Expense 118
Adding a New Entry 119
Expense Type 121
Expense Amount 121
Viewing Receipt Details 121

CONTENTS   vii

Add a Note to an Entry 128
Menu Commands 128

11 APPLICATIONS—CALCULATOR   133

Using the Calculator 133
Addition 135
Subtraction 135
Multiplication 136
Division...136
Additional Function Keys...137
Menu Commands 138

12 APPLICATIONS—MAIL   141

Using the Mail Application..141
Menu Commands 147

13 APPLICATIONS—SECURITY   155

Using the Security Features 155
Assigning a Password 157

14 ADDITIONAL PALM PROGRAMS AND UTILITIES   161

More Palm Programs 161
Find 161
Menu Commands—Edit 163
Checking the Memory Status of Your Palm 165
Menu Commands—Main Applications Screen 167
Menu Commands—Main Applications Screen—Options 168
Giraffe Game...169

15 INITIAL PC HARDWARE AND SOFTWARE SETUP   171

Setting Up Your Hardware 171
Connecting the HotSync Cradle 172

16	**DESKTOP SOFTWARE—ADDRESS BOOK**	**177**
	Opening the Address Book 177	
	Adding a New Entry 179	
	Viewing an Existing Entry 182	
	Find an Existing Entry 182	
	Categories 183	

17	**DESKTOP APPLICATIONS—DATE BOOK**	**186**
	What Is the Desktop Date Book? 186	
	Adding a New Entry 190	
	View an Existing Event...194	
	Accessing the Address Book and To Do List 196	

18	**DESKTOP SOFTWARE—TO DO LIST**	**200**
	What Is the To Do List? 200	
	Opening the To Do List Program 200	
	Adding a New Entry 202	
	Show To Do Preferences..205	

19	**DESKTOP SOFTWARE—MEMO PAD**	**207**
	What Is the Memo Pad? 207	
	Starting the Memo Pad Program...208	
	Adding a New Entry 209	
	Viewing an Existing Entry 210	
	Changing Memo Details 211	
	Deleting a Memo Pad Item...211	

20	**HOW TO HOTSYNC**	**213**
	Synchronizing Data with HotSync 213	
	HotSyncing from Your Palm...214	
	Starting the HotSync Manager from Your PC 216	
	Setting Up the HotSync Manager from the Palm Desktop 217	

21 ADDING A NEW APPLICATION TO YOUR PALM   220

Starting the Install Tool..221
Installing New Programs...222
Deleting Programs 223

A   LIST OF SUGGESTED WEB SITES   225

Hardware...225
User Groups 225
Resellers 226
Informational..226
Software (Desktop Personal Information Managers
    that can HotSync with the Palm)..........................227

INDEX   229

Acknowledgments

My thanks to my family and friends for all their support and help during the creation this book.

Special thanks to Steve Isenberg and Evie Tse, my friends and New England Palm Users Group co-founders, for their invaluable assistance and patience.

Finally, my sincere thanks to my acquisitions editor Renee Wilmeth for giving me this opportunity and all her help.

Trademarks

All terms mentioned in this book that are known to be trademarks or service marks have been appropriately capitalized. Sams Publishing cannot attest to the accuracy of this information. Use of a term in this book should not be regarded as affecting the validity of any trademark or service mark.

About the Author

Michael Steinberg is a Technology Marketing Consultant. He is also the president and co-founder of the New England Palm Users Group based in Boston.

Michael has more than 15 years' experience as a computer marketing professional. Prior to becoming a consultant, he held sales and product marketing positions at several computer and technology marketing companies.

Michael is also an experienced business traveler. In his spare time he operates an informational web site to aid his fellow road warriors. He has covered hundreds of thousands of miles, making numerous presentations to large corporate accounts, trade shows, conferences, and computer user groups. It was this heavy travel schedule, combined with a keen interest in technology, that led him to purchase a 3Com PalmPilot in 1997.

Early in 1998, Michael co-founded the New England Palm Users Group to provide an educational resource to owners (and would-be owners) of the 3Com PalmPilot and IBM WorkPad.

Michael can be reached through his web site at **http://www.Business-Trip.com**.

The New England Palm Users Group can be reached through their web site at **http:/www.NE-Palm.org**.

Tell Us What You Think

As a reader, you are the most important critic and commentator of our books. We value your opinion and want to know what we're doing right, what we could do better, what areas you'd like to see us publish in, and any other words of wisdom you're willing to pass our way. You can help us make strong books that meet your needs and give you the computer guidance you require.

If you have access to the World Wide Web, check out our site at **http://www.mcp.com**. If you have a technical question about this book, call the technical support line at (317) 581-3833 or send email to **support@mcp.com**.

Your comments will help us to continue publishing the best books available on computer topics in today's market. You can contact us at

Publisher
Sams Publishing
201 West 103rd Street
Indianapolis, Indiana 46290
USA

Introduction

What Is Teach Yourself PalmPilot and Palm III in 10 Minutes?

This series takes a different approach to teaching people how to use a computer program. We do not attempt to cover every detail of the program. Instead, each book concentrates on the program features that are essential for most users, the features that you need to get your work done. Our goal is to teach you, as quickly and painlessly as possible, those things you need to start using your PalmPilot or Palm III and get the most value from it.

Using This Book

Teach Yourself PalmPilot and Palm III in 10 Minutes contains a total of 21 lessons. Ideally, you should work through them in order.

Several special elements are used throughout the book to highlight specific types of information.

> **Timesaver Tip** These tips offer shortcuts and hints for using PalmPilot and Palm III most effectively.

> **Plain English** These identify new terms and definitions.

> **Panic Button** These appear in places where new users often run into trouble.

Several other of the book's features are designed to make your learning faster and easier:

- Numbered steps provide exact instructions for commonly needed procedures.
- Menu commands, toolbar buttons, and dialog box options that you select are printed in blue for easy recognition.
- Text that you enter is **boldface and blue.**
- Messages that appear on-screen are **boldface.**

Lesson 1

Getting to Know Your Palm Organizer

In this lesson, you learn how to turn on the Palm and adjust the contrast.

Congratulations! You have chosen the Palm handheld computer, a well-designed Personal Digital Assistant (or PDA) that will help make you more productive as well as save several extra pounds of weight.

Why the Palm? Maybe, like me, a colleague or friend gave you a demonstration and you were hooked. Maybe you are tired of carrying that bulky, paper daily planner back and forth to work everyday. Maybe you like the idea of having your vital personal information easily accessible and constantly backed up. Maybe you have forgotten one too many birthday cards. Whatever your reason, you made the right choice.

You will be pleasantly surprised at how easy it is to use. So what do you do now? Just think, in a very short time you could be

- Adding that next important client meeting to your calendar
- Creating a supermarket shopping list
- Making a reminder to pick up flowers and make dinner reservations for you anniversary
- Writing a summary of a critical conference call for distribution to the sales team
- Looking up the date of your last haircut
- Forwarding the email from your top prospect to everyone in the company, congratulating everyone for being awarded the huge project they have been working on for months

- Entering in a dinner receipt from your latest business trip
- Looking at the value of your stock portfolio on the Internet
- Reading a recent bestseller

Or any of the thousands of other potential uses for your Palm.

What's next? Read this book, of course.

What are you waiting for? Let's get going.

> **PDA** PDA stands for Personal Digital Assistant. A PDA is an electronic device designed to help you with everyday tasks, enabling you to me more efficient. A PDA can be any brand of handheld computer. Most enable you to add various kinds of software and some even let you program.

Choosing a Palm Computer

Before we start, let's take a minute to discuss the history of the products and some of the features of the two Palm models covered in this book—The PalmPilot Professional Edition and the Palm III.

In 1996, Palm Computing released its first products, the Pilot 1000 and 5000 series.

The PalmPilot Professional Edition came out in 1997 (along with a lower-priced counterpart, the PalmPilot Personal, which offered less memory).

The PalmPilot Professional Edition feature list includes the following:

- A light, easy-to-handle hardware product, small enough to fit in the palm of your hand or in your shirt pocket
- Backlight and contrast control
- "Hard" application buttons located on the front, for quick start of your most popular programs
- Palm OS 2.0 (the operating system), offering a full set of applications (Address Book, Date Book, To Do List, and so on)

- A HotSync cradle, used to connect the Palm to your PC
- 1MB of memory
- Palm Desktop software

In 1997, IBM also began selling a licensed version of the PalmPilot Professional under the name WorkPad.

The Palm III was introduced in 1998. It offered the same features as the PalmPilot Professional, as well as the following:

- A new sleeker unit design
- Palm OS 3.0
- 2MB of memory
- Infrared beaming, for sending data between Palm units

IBM also offers a version of this product. In addition, Palm Computing was offering an upgrade (or field retrofit) kit for PalmPilot Professional owners. The upgrade included a 1MB memory upgrade, infrared beam technology, and Palm OS 3.0.

You have your Palm in your hand (pardon the bad pun). What do you do now? First, let's talk about the actual unit. This lesson covers the basic operations of your Palm:turning on the power, using the hard application buttons, using the backlight, and adjusting the contrast control.

> **Handle with Care** Although the folks at Palm Computing did an excellent job designing the Palm, it is generally agreed that the plastic casing of the PalmPilot Professional is not quite as solid as one might expect. Be sure and handle the PalmPilot carefully. The casing on the Palm III is thought to be more rugged.

Quick Tour

The following diagrams show the front and rear layout of your Palm. Note the slight variations in design between the PalmPilot and the Palm III.

As you look at the front of your unit, locate the following:

- Power switch
- Hard application buttons
- Page Up/Down buttons
- Main display
- Soft application buttons
- Graffiti pad
- Stylus

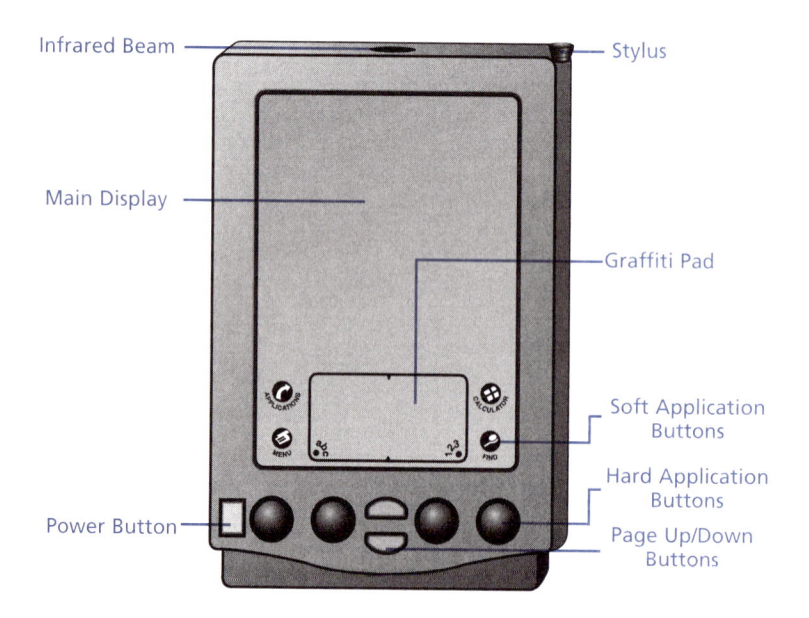

FIGURE 1.1 The front view.

As you view the rear and side of your unit, locate the following:

GETTING TO KNOW YOUR PALM ORGANIZER 5

- Contrast control
- Battery compartment door
- Memory compartment door
- Reset button
- Serial port

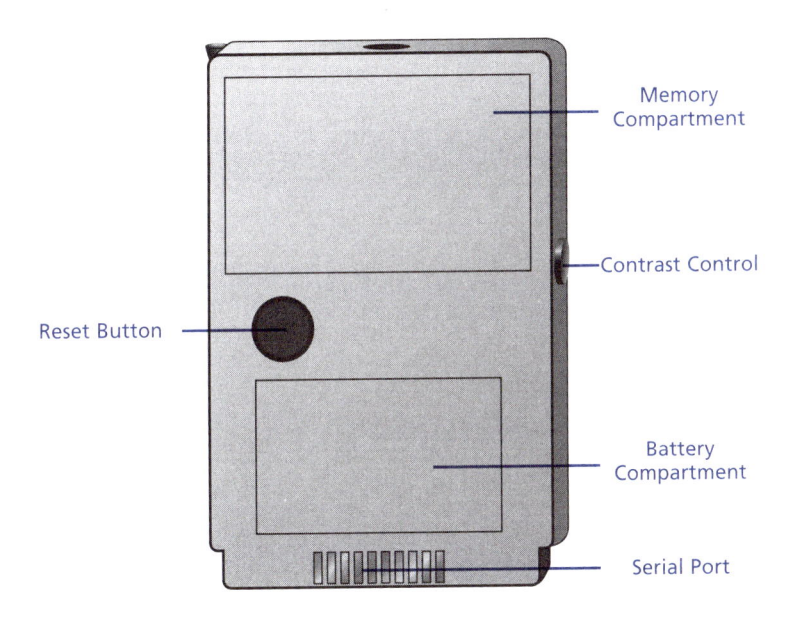

FIGURE 1.2 The rear view.

The use of all these is explained in the next few lessons.

STARTING UP

There are two main ways to start your Palm:

- The main power switch
- A "hard" application-specific button, if you are looking for specific information very quickly

USING THE POWER SWITCH

The power switch is the light-green button located on the lower-left front of the Palm (refer to Figure 1.1). The button is embossed with a figure of the sun. To start the Palm, press the power switch down once. The display will normally show the last screen in use prior to the Palm being turned off.

> **Power to the...Palm!** The Palm is not going to do you much good without batteries. Make sure you have a fresh set of two AAA batteries in the Palm before continuing with this lesson.

USING THE APPLICATION-SPECIFIC BUTTONS

Four circular application-specific startup buttons are located at the bottom of the front of the Palm (refer to Figure 1.2). These start up each application individually, if you haven't already used the overall power start.

Each button is marked with one of the following icons:

BUTTON	BUTTON NAME
Date Book	Date Book
Address	Address Book icon
To Do List	To Do List icon
Memo Pad	Memo Pad icon

If you wish to start a specific application immediately, press the specific button for that application once. The display will show the last screen in use for that particular application. Using the hard buttons turns the Palm on automatically.

> **Quick Start!** The application-specific buttons can also be used if the Palm is already powered on. Doing so can save you several steps.
>
> You can reprogram the application-specific buttons for use with other applications. Lesson 5 covers that topic.

DISPLAYING THE BACKLIGHT

Your Palm display is equipped with a backlight feature. The backlight can be useful if the display cannot be easily viewed with available light.

To activate the backlight, follow these steps

1. Press the power switch and hold the button down for approximately three seconds. Note: It does not matter if the unit is already powered on.

2. The backlight appears.

> **Power Drain** As you might expect, continuous use of the backlight will drain the batteries that much faster.

ADJUSTING THE CONTRAST

In addition to backlighting, the Palm is also equipped with a contrast control. This control adjusts the actual screen display, making it lighter or darker. The contrast control is a small wheel located on the left edge of the Palm. All this and it glows in the dark too!

To adjust the contrast, follow these steps:

1. Power on the Palm.

2. Gently turn the wheel on the side of the case up or down until you can read the display comfortably.

Well, those are a few of the hardware basics you will use on a regular basis.

> **Mirror, Mirror on the Palm** The main display is designed to be very reflective for easier viewing. What most people don't notice is that it can double as a personal mirror in a pinch. Check it out. What will they think of next.

In this lesson, you learned the layout and basic hardware operations of your Palm. In the next lesson, you learn about some additional hardware elements you need to be aware of.

Lesson 2

More Hardware Operations

In this lesson, you learn how to work with the stylus, reset the system, add memory, and change the batteries in your Palm computer.

Removing the Stylus

To maneuver around the main display or enter data directly into the Palm, you use the stylus. The stylus is a long, slender piece of plastic, shaped like a pen. It is normally stored in a holder on the right side of the Palm unit, in a section specifically designed for it.

To remove the stylus, follow these steps:

1. Hold the Palm firmly in one hand, with the right side of the unit facing you.

2. With your other hand, place your thumb gently on the exposed ridges at the top of the stylus and your index finger at the top-right corner of the Palm for leverage.

3. Use your thumb to slide the stylus upward and remove it from the holder.

Replacing the Stylus in the Holder

To replace the stylus in the holder, follow these steps:

1. Gently slide it downward so that the exposed ridges at the top face you.

2. Slide the stylus into the holder until you hear a click. This sound indicates the stylus is now locked into place.

It is common to lose the stylus. You may wish to keep an extra stylus or two available. You can purchase a variety of them.

> **Get the Point?** Replacement styluses are available from Palm Computing and a variety of third-party vendors. Contact your Palm Products reseller, local computer users group, or search the Internet for additional information.

> **Finger Pointing!** You can use your fingertip to maneuver around the main display, but be sure to keep the display clean.

> **No Sharp Objects!** Do not use a pencil, the open tip of a regular pen, or other sharp object on the main display. It can seriously damage the display. Use a stylus.

CHANGING THE BATTERIES IN YOUR PALM COMPUTER

The Palm requires two AAA batteries to operate. The battery compartment is located on the back of the unit on the lower-right side (see Figure 2.1).

MORE HARDWARE OPERATIONS   11

Battery
Compartment

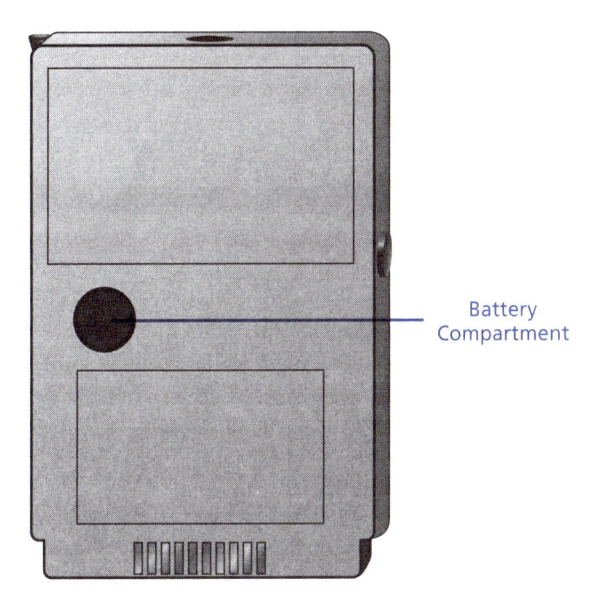

FIGURE 2.1   The battery compartment.

To change the batteries, follow these steps:

1. Open the battery compartment by locating the grooved area on the battery compartment door.

2. With one quick motion, place your thumb on the grooved area and push down with gentle pressure.

3. At the same time, slide and remove the compartment door to the right.

> Note that steps 2 and 3 apply only to the PalmPilot Professional. The Palm III battery door has a easy-open latch, and the door swings open while still connected to your unit.

4. Lift the old batteries out of the exposed battery compartment.

5. Remove the old batteries. Gently place the new batteries in each slot, following the diagram inside the compartment.

6. After the batteries are in place, gently slide the door back over the compartment until you hear a click. This sound indicates the door is now locked in place. For the Palm III, close the door until it locks.

> **A Timed Event (or Timing Is Everything)** The Palm comes equipped with a small battery backup for the memory. You must change the batteries within one minute; otherwise you will lose all of your data.

RESETTING THE SYSTEM

On very rare occasions, your Palm may develop a software or hardware problem. For this or some other reason, you may be instructed to **Reset the Palm**. Resetting the Palm is similar to restarting your personal computer. It will not hurt the operation of the unit, if done properly.

> **Back Up, Back Up, Back Up!** Backing up (or performing a hotsync in Palm terminology) is a very important aspect of being a Palm owner. When you synchronize with the hotsync procedure, you place an exact copy of your data on both your Palm and PC. Although you learn more about hotsync in a later lesson, I can't stress enough that you should back up your Palm prior to performing a reset.

There are three types of resets:
- *The soft reset*. Reboots only, no data lost.
- *The warm (or semisoft) reset*. Removes all outside programs from the system, in the belief that they are causing the problem. You lose only the data associated with these programs.
- *The hard reset*. Complete system reset. You lose all data.

Soft Reset

A soft reset tells the unit to clear its basic memory and start up again. The data you have entered or hotsynced previously will be saved.

To perform a soft reset follow these steps:

1. Hold the unit face down in the palm of one hand.
2. Locate the Reset button hole located on the back of the unit (see Figure 2.2).

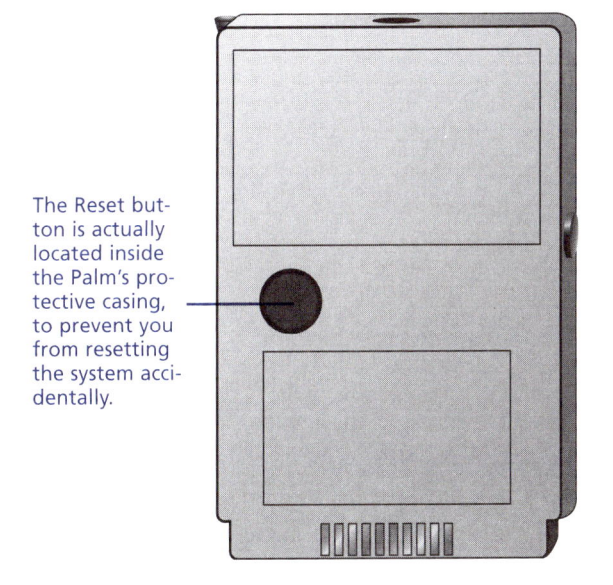

The Reset button is actually located inside the Palm's protective casing, to prevent you from resetting the system accidentally.

FIGURE 2.2   The Reset button.

3. Using a paperclip (or similar device that does not have a sharp end), slide the end of the paperclip into the Reset button hole *very* carefully until it stops.
4. Push down once *very* gently. You will feel slight pressure as you press the button and hear a small click.

5. Remove the paperclip from the hole.

6. Carefully turn the unit over. The main display changes. This indicates that the unit has successfully reset.

> **Built-In Paperclip?** Not exactly, but if you remove the tip from the end of the Palm III stylus, you will find a blunt end you can use for resets. However, you should *never* use this blunt end for data entry.

> **Why So Difficult?** The Reset button is actually located inside the Palm's protective casing, so that you will not reset the system accidentally.

If your problem has not cleared, perform a warm reset.

WARM RESET

A warm reset removes any program outside of the base Palm OS. These programs can occasionally cause system problems, so removing only them may enable you to operate normally.

To perform a warm reset, follow these steps:

1. Push down and hold the Page Up button located at the lower front of the unit.

2. With this button held down, turn the unit over and gently place the end of the paperclip into the Reset button, pressing once lightly.

3. The system should then reset.

If your problem has not cleared, perform a hard reset.

HARD RESET

A hard reset clears the *entire* system. This means all data entered into the system will be lost. However, the base OS, including the resident applications, will remain. This should only be performed if a soft and warm reset fail to clear your problem.

> **Only a Last Resort** You should only perform a hard reset if a soft and warm reset do not clear up a problem. Remember that a hard reset will clear all entered data into your Palm.

To perform a hard reset, follow these steps:

1. Hold the unit face down in the palm of one hand and locate the Reset button hole on the back of the unit (refer to Figure 2.2).

2. Using that same hand, push the Power button on the front of the unit and hold it down.

3. Using a paperclip (or similar device that does not have sharp end), slide the end of the paperclip into the Reset button hole *very* carefully until it stops.

4. Push down once *very* gently. You will feel slight pressure as you press the button and hear a small click. Remove the paperclip from the hole. If you carefully turn the unit over, you will see the main display change.

5. The display will now tell you that you are about to erase all data stored on the Palm.

6. Press the Page Up button on the front of the unit. This erases all the data and resets the unit to factory default.

    Or...

    Press any other button on the front of the unit. This aborts the hard reset and performs a soft reset as described previously.

Adding Memory

Your Palm is equipped with 1MB of memory in the PalmPilot Professional and 2MB in the Palm III. Each unit is designed to hold additional memory. You can purchase additional memory modules from 3Com/Palm Computing or from a third-party vendor.

The memory compartment is located on the rear of the unit at the top. To add additional memory, follow the memory manufacturer's instructions *exactly*. This will reduce the risk of damaging your unit.

> **Memory Can Help** Watch your unit's memory status (how to do so is covered in a later lesson). The base memory that comes with your unit should be enough to handle your typical daily requirements. If you plan to use a large number of applications or store large amounts of data, however, consider upgrading your memory.

In this lesson, you learned how to change the battery, reset your Palm computer and assess whether you need additional memory. In the next lesson, you start working with the software by getting a feel for how to maneuver the main display.

Lesson 3

Maneuvering the Main Display

In this lesson, you learn how to move around the main display of your PalmPilot Professional Edition or Palm III connected organizer.

What is the main display?

The main display on your Palm is where you will enter and view your data. You will want to get used to the layout of the display so that you can use your Palm most efficiently.

Now that you have learned how to operate the basic hardware, you are ready to start using the Palm. Let's start with maneuvering the main display.

Touring the Main Display

The main display is located on the front of the Palm (see Figure 3.1). It is made up of two main sections:

18 LESSON 3

FIGURE 3.1 The Palm's main display.

- The lower portion of the display contains several "soft" application buttons and the Graffiti data entry area.
- The upper portion of the display is the primary display screen.

> **Soft Buttons** A "soft" button is attached to a computer input device, like the front screen of the Palm unit. When pressed, a soft button performs a specific function, such as starting an application.

SOFT BUTTONS

The lower portion of the front on the Palm contains four soft application buttons, each with an icon. Each application button will bring up its own menu screen or entry screen. The four main buttons and their icons are as follows:

Applications icon

Menu icon

MANEUVERING THE MAIN DISPLAY   19

Calculator icon

Find icon

Unlike the hard application-specific buttons discussed in the preceding lesson, the soft buttons function only when the Palm is powered "on." Let's discuss the function of each button in more detail.

APPLICATIONS

The Applications button brings up the main menu of the Palm. The main menu lists all the applications that reside on the Palm. (If you add software to your Palm, it will show up here.) This is the most common display for the Palm, because it enables you to access any other application.

To select the Applications button, follow these steps:

1. Turn on the Palm.
2. Using the stylus, gently tap the Applications soft button once.
3. The Applications main menu should appear (see Figure 3.2).

FIGURE 3.2   Applications main menu (also called an Application Picker).

> **Previous Use (Palm OS 2.0)** Depending on the preceding use, the main menu may already be on the display when you power on the unit. If so, when you tap the Applications button, it will bring up the Preferences menu. We discuss the Preferences menu in another section. Gently tap the Applications button one more time. The main menu should now be on the display.

> **Third-Party Software** Several vendors offer software that also acts as Application Pickers. Check with your Palm Product reseller, local Palm users group, or on the Internet for additional information.

CALCULATOR

Your Palm is equipped with a full-function calculator. (We discuss the operation of the calculator in a later lesson.)

To access the calculator, follow these steps:

1. Turn on the Palm.
2. Using the stylus, gently tap the Calculator soft button once.
3. The Calculator main screen should appear (see Figure 3.3).

MANEUVERING THE MAIN DISPLAY   21

FIGURE 3.3   Calculator.

To get to the Applications main menu from the calculator, tap the Applications soft button once. The main menu screen should then appear.

MENU

The Menu soft button gives you access to pull-down menus associated with many of the Palm applications. These pull-down menus can offer a variety of additional functionality, depending on the specific application in use. (We discuss the functions of each pull-down menu in detail when we cover each application.) To use the Menu button, you must be in an application. Here, we try it with the calculator.

To access the Menu display, follow these steps:

1. Turn on the Palm.

2. Using the stylus, gently tap the Calculator soft button once. The Calculator main screen should appear.

3. Tap the Menu soft button once. A pull-down menu bar with the words **Edit** and **Options** should appear at the top of the main display (see Figure 3.4), with the Edit menu open.

22 LESSON 3

FIGURE 3.4   Pull-down menu bar.

4. Tap the pull-down menu bar. The Edit menu should close (see Figure 3.5).

FIGURE 3.5   The Edit menu is closed.

5. Tap the **Menu** soft button again. The pull-down menu should close, leaving the Calculator main screen (see Figure 3.6).

FIGURE 3.6 Back to Calculator screen.

6. Tap the Applications soft button. The main menu should appear (see Figure 3.7).

FIGURE 3.7 Back to the main menu.

FIND

The Find soft button, represented by the magnifying glass icon, is another useful main display button. Find can be a useful application when you are trying to locate a specific piece of data, such as a person, company, city, or event name.

Because we have not yet covered data entry, we will discuss Find in more detail in another lesson. For now, however, here's a basic lesson (specific to Palm OS 3.01).

To use Find, follow these steps:

1. Turn on the Palm. The main menu should be on the display.
2. Tap the Find soft button once. The main Find screen appears (see Figure 3.8), located at the bottom of the display.

FIGURE 3.8   The main Find screen.

3. Tap the Cancel button. The Find screen should disappear, leaving on the main Applications screen.

> Note that in Palm OS 2.0, when you tap Find, the last application you had open should come up first. In our case, it will be the Calculator screen, accompanied by the main Find screen, which appears at the bottom of the display.

> **Cancel** The Cancel button on the Palm display is used when you want to exit an application or other activity without saving changes. When in doubt, using the Cancel button is a safe move.

BATTERY INDICATOR

As long as we are talking about the main display, I should mention the battery-level indicator.

The battery-level indicator is located at the top of the display in Palm OS 3.0 (see Figure 3.9) and at the bottom of the display in Palm OS 2.0.

FIGURE 3.9   Battery-level indicator.

It will go from solid to white as your battery power level decreases. You will receive a warning prior to the battery level reaching zero.

In this lesson, you learned how to get around the Palm display, as well as how to open some applications. In the next lesson, you learn how to actually enter data into your Palm.

Lesson 4

Manual Data Entry

In this lesson, you learn how to enter data by hand into your Palm.

So far, we have covered the basic hardware operation and how to maneuver around the main display. To be most productive, however, you need to enter phone numbers, meetings, and other vital information. You can enter data via your computer in a process called *hotsyncing* (which is covered later). In this lesson, you learn about inputting information by hand. When it comes to making it easy, the folks at Palm Computing really did their homework. Entering data manually is actually easier than you might think.

The manufacturer of the Palm has provided the following two ways to manually enter data directly into your Palm:

- Graffiti, Palm's handwriting recognition system
- An onscreen keyboard

Entering Data with Graffiti

Graffiti is Palm's handwriting recognition system. Using the stylus, you "write" the entry one character at a time on the Graffiti data entry pad, using Graffiti's data entry guides (see Figures 4.1–4.7). You print each character in a manner similar to printing it on a piece of paper. The Graffiti data entry pad is located on the lower section of the main display (see Figure 4.7).

LESSON 4

FIGURE 4.1 Graffiti Help: numbers and letters.

FIGURE 4.2 Graffiti Help: space, back space, and so on.

FIGURE 4.3 Graffiti Help: punctuation, additional characters, and so on.

MANUAL DATA ENTRY   29

FIGURE **4.4**   Graffiti Help: additional characters.

FIGURE **4.5**   Additional characters.

FIGURE **4.6**   Additional characters.

FIGURE 4.7 Graffiti data entry pad.

Here are some important notes about Graffiti:

- Pay particular attention to the Graffiti entry guide. Each character has a black dot. This dot indicates where to start entering the character. Don't draw the dot, just use it as a guide.
- When using the Graffiti data entry pad, remember to enter letters on the left side of the pad and numbers on the right side.
- Graffiti has been designed so that each entry is one "stroke". Every standard keyboard character is available. You will get the best performance by making sure you keep the stylus in full contact with the pad when making the entry.

> **Be Gentle** Like the display, the Graffiti pad is made to take normal wear and tear. You can extend the life of the pad, however, by not applying heavy pressure when entering strokes. Practice and you will see that light pressure works just fine.

When you first look at the data entry guide on the back of the unit, you might think Graffiti is somewhat difficult to use. After you get used to it, however, it almost becomes second nature.

Learning Graffiti

The easiest way to learn and practice the Graffiti entry language is to play a simple game called Giraffe. Giraffe comes installed on your Palm and requires you to enter Graffiti strokes to play. Experienced users report that 20 minutes with Giraffe is usually all you need to become proficient in Graffiti.

To open and play Giraffe, follow these steps:

1. Turn on the Palm.
2. Tap the Applications soft button. The Applications Picker menu appears.
3. Tap the Giraffe game icon. The opening screen for the game appears.
4. Follow the instructions.

Entering Data with the Onscreen Keyboard

Your Palm is also equipped with an onscreen keyboard (sometime referred to as a "soft" keyboard). You can use this keyboard in conjunction with or as a replacement to Graffiti.

The Palm actually has three onscreen keyboards:

- Letters (see Figure 4.8)
- Numbers and extended characters (see Figure 4.9)
- International characters (see Figure 4.10)

FIGURE 4.8 Onscreen keyboard: letters.

FIGURE 4.9 Onscreen keyboard: numbers.

FIGURE 4.10   Onscreen keyboard: international characters.

Bringing Up the Onscreen Keyboard

You can bring the onscreen keyboard to the main display in the following three ways:

- Tapping on the Graffiti entry keypad
- Using the Menu soft button
- Using a special tap sequence going from the Graffiti pad to the main display

You need to be in an application to bring up the different keyboards.

From the Graffiti Entry Pad

While in your data entry application (for example Memo Pad), you can make the keyboard appear by following these steps:

1. Tap the lower-left or right corner of the Graffiti entry pad (depending on whether you want the letters or numbers keyboard.)

2. On the lower-left corner, you will see a dot with the letters **abc**. Tap this dot once to bring up the letters keyboard.

34   Lesson 4

3. On the lower-right corner, you will see a dot with the numbers **123**. Tap this dot once to bring up the numbers and extended characters keyboard.

Using the Menu Soft Button

While in your data entry application (for example Memo Pad), you can make the keyboard appear by following these steps:

1. Tap the Menu soft button once. A pull-down menu bar will appear at the top of the screen (see Figure 4.11).

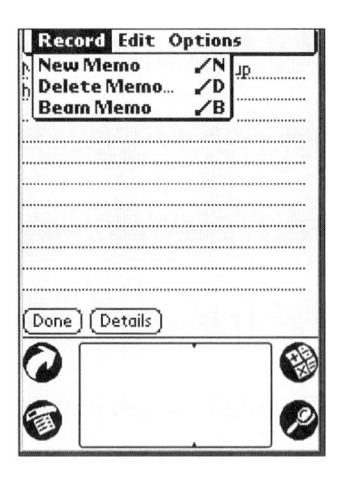

Figure 4.11   Pull-down menu bar.

2. Tap Edit. The Edit pull-down menu appears (see Figure 4.12).

MANUAL DATA ENTRY   35

```
    Record  Edit  Options
New England  Undo        ✓U
http://www   Cut         ✓X
             Copy        ✓C
             Paste       ✓P
             Select All  ✓S
             Keyboard    ✓K
             Graffiti Help ✓G


  (Done) (Details)
```

FIGURE 4.12   Edit menu.

3. Tap Keyboard. The letters keyboard will appear.

USING A SPECIAL STYLUS SEQUENCE

While in your data entry application for example Memo Pad), you can make the keyboard appear by following these steps:

1. Place your stylus on the Graffiti pad.

2. Then in one continuous motion, move the stylus across the pad onto the main display screen and lift the stylus off the screen.

3. If you start from the left side of the Graffiti pad, the letters keyboard will appear. If you start from the right side, the numbers keyboard will appear. Note: This is the only method to access the numbers keyboard directly. The other methods always bring up the letters keyboard first.

> **Hey, I Can't Make That Last One Work!** To use the special tap sequence, you must specify it in Preferences, Buttons, Pen. See Lesson 5, "Maximizing Your Palm—Preferences and Applications," for details.

Enter a Character

To enter a character, just tap that character on the keyboard.

> **Tap Protection** The main display screen will last longer if you tap gently. In addition, third-party vendors offer adhesive plastic covers that also protect the screen.

Change Keyboards

To change from one keyboard to another, tap on the appropriate key at the bottom of the keyboard:

- **abc** ñ Letters
- **123** ñ Numeric
- **Intl** ñ International

Remove the Keyboard

To remove the keyboard from the screen, tap the Done key. The keyboard will disappear.

Online Tips

The Palm OS includes online tips to help you with particular functions such as entering text or locating menus. To view a tip, look for an **i** at the top of the main display (see Figure 4.13). Tap the i to view the tip.

Memo Details

FIGURE 4.13 Sample tip screen.

If the online tip is longer than one screen, tap the page-down arrow located at the lower-right side of the screen. When you are done viewing the tip, tap Done.

> **More Data Entry Options** In addition to Graffiti and the Palm soft keyboard, several third-party vendors offer software and hardware products for manually entering data. Check with your Palm products reseller, a local Palm users group, or the Internet for more information.

In this lesson, you learned how to enter data using both Graffiti and the Palm soft keyboard. You have also been learning how to access the onscreen keyboard in several ways and enter text. In the next lesson, you set up your preferences.

Lesson 5

Maximizing Your Palm—Preferences and Applications

In this lesson, you learn how to set the preferences in your Palm.

Preferences are internal settings or other information for your Palm. There are two main types of preferences—primary and secondary. Primary preferences are items such as the correct date and time. This information is vital if your Palm is to operate properly. Secondary preferences are items such as shortcuts for entering data. This type of information can make your use of the Palm more efficient.

> **Everyone Is Different** The reason this lesson is fairly long is because the Palm has a wide variety of preferences available for you to set. We all have individual needs. I strongly recommend that you check each preference setting at least once.

Preferences

Now you are ready to start maximizing your Palm. The first thing to do is set your preferences. These settings tell your Palm how to operate. The Preferences section has the following eight categories:

- General
- Buttons
- Digitizer
- Formats
- Modem
- Network
- Owner
- ShortCuts

Let's step through each category. You can then set the individual preferences to meet your specific needs.

GETTING TO THE PREFERENCES MENU

To reach the Preferences menu, follow these steps:

1. From the Main menu, tap the Preferences icon.
2. The Category list is located in the upper-right corner of the main display (see Figure 5.1).
3. Tap the list to view the full list (see Figure 5.2).
4. Tap General.

FIGURE 5.1 Category list location.

FIGURE 5.2 Full category list.

Palm Applications, Preferences, General

You are now looking at the Main General Preferences screen (see Figure 5.3). The following general preferences are available:

FIGURE 5.3   Main General Preferences screen.

- Set Time
- Set Date
- Auto-off after
- System Sound
- Alarm Sound
- Game Sound
- Beam Receive

Let's step through each one.

SET TIME

To set the current time, follow these steps:

1. Tap the box that contains the time. You are now viewing the Time entry screen (see Figure 5.4).

FIGURE 5.4   Time entry screen.

  2. To set the hour, tap the hour indicator.
  3. Use the up/down arrows to the right to move to the correct number.
  4. Repeat these steps to set the minutes.
  5. To select AM or PM, just tap on the appropriate choice located to the right of the up/down arrows.
  6. When the correct time appears, tap OK.
  7. To cancel your entry, tap Cancel.

SET DATE

To set the current date, follow these steps:

  1. Tap the box that contains the date. You are now viewing the Date entry screen (see Figure 5. 5).

MAXIMIZING YOUR PALM—PREFERENCES AND APPLICATIONS 43

FIGURE 5.5 Date entry screen.

2. If the current settings are correct, tap Today. The application will automatically return to the main General Preferences screen.

3. To select the year, use the right/left arrows located on each side of the year displayed at the top of the screen, until the correct year appears.

4. To select the month, tap the correct month from the list that appears below the year indicator.

5. To select the day, tap the correct day from the list displayed below the month list. When you select the day, the application will automatically return to the main General Preferences screen.

> **Cancel** If at anytime you wish to end the entry without saving changes, tap Cancel. The application will automatically return to the main General Preferences screen.

> **What Time Is It?** It is very important to keep the Date and Time setting accurate. These settings are used by the Date Book application Alarm system. If improperly set, you could miss an important reminder.

AUTO-OFF AFTER

Auto-off after is a utility that automatically shuts off your Palm after a specified amount of inactivity. It is designed to extend the life of your batteries.

To change the setting, follow these steps:

1. Tap on the existing setting.
2. Tap on your new choice: 1, 2, or 3 minutes.

SYSTEM SOUND

Your Palm will make a sound when you perform certain activities, such as when you tap on a soft application button. You can decide the level of the sound. To change the sound level, tap on the existing selection. Choose a new level from the list provided: Off, High, Medium, or Low.

> **Palm 2.0 Systems** If your are using Palm OS 2.0, you will only have a check box that will enable or disable the sound.

ALARM SOUND

Your Palm will sound an alarm if/when you designate such as to remind you about a event or anniversary. You can decide the level of the sound. To change the sound level, tap on the existing selection. Choose a new level from the list provided: Off, High, Medium, or Low.

> **Palm 2.0 Systems** If your are using Palm OS 2.0, you will only have a check box that will enable or disable the sound.

Game Sound

Your Palm will make a sound when you play certain games. You can adjust the level of the sound.

To change the sound level, follow these steps:

1. Tap on the existing selection.
2. Choose a new level from the list provided: Off, High, Medium, or Low.

> **Palm 2.0 Systems** If you are using Palm OS 2.0, you will only have a check box that will enable or disable the sound.

Beam Receive

If your Palm is equipped with an infrared beam, turning the setting to ON will allow your unit to automatically receive data from another Palm.

Palm Applications, Preferences, Buttons

You have the option to reprogram the applications associated with each of the hard application buttons (located at the bottom front of your Palm), as well as the Calculator soft button (located at the lower portion of the main display, next to the Graffiti Pad).

To change how the buttons are associated, follow these steps:

1. Go to the category list (**General** is displayed), located in the upper-right corner of the main display (see Figure 5.6).

```
Preferences         ▼ General
    Set Time: 1:03 pm
    Set Date: 8/11/98
```

FIGURE 5.6 Category list.

2. Tap the list to view the full list (see Figure 5.7).

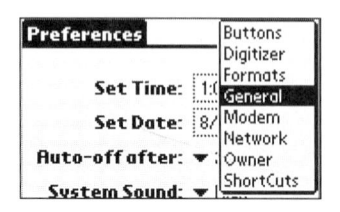

```
Preferences         Buttons
                    Digitizer
                    Formats
    Set Time: 1:0 General
    Set Date: 8/  Modem
                    Network
 Auto-off after: ▼  Owner
                    ShortCuts
 System Sound: ▼
```

FIGURE 5.7 Full category list.

3. Tap Buttons. You are now looking at the main Buttons Preferences screen (see Figure 5.8).

```
Preferences         ▼ Buttons
Select an application to
customize each button:

  ▼ Date Book
              ▼ Memo Pad
  ▼ Address
              ▼ Calc
  ▼ To Do List

(Default) (Pen...) (HotSync...)
```

Figure 5.8 Main Buttons Preferences screen.

If you wish to change the application associated with a given button, tap the application name next to that button. A list of all available applications will appear (see Figure 5.9). Tap the new application you wish to be associated with that particular button. Repeat these steps for each button you wish to change.

4. Repeat these steps for each button you wish to change.

FIGURE 5.9   Available applications list.

> **Button It and Save Time!**   If you plan to use a particular application on a regular basis, you may want to reprogram one of these buttons to start it on command. Doing so saves you several steps (Turning on the power, accessing the Application Picker, and selecting the application).

DEFAULT SETTINGS

You may establish default settings for your buttons. After you have decided on your defaults, tap Default. This locks these settings into memory.

You may then change your settings temporarily to suit a particular need. After you have finished, just tap Default and the settings will automatically return to your default settings.

Let me give you an example. I going to presume that all the buttons are set the way they came from the factory. You decide that because you use the calculator all the time. To make this swap, follow these steps:

1. Turn on the Palm.

2. Tap the Applications soft button; this brings up the Application Picker screen.

3. Tap the Preferences icon. This brings up the last Preference screen you worked with.

4. In the upper-right corner of the display, the name of the Preference screen you are on appears (probably **General**) with a down arrow to the right. Tap that name. This brings up the complete preference list.

5. Tap Buttons. This brings up the Buttons Preferences screen.

6. The To Do List icon is on the left side of the display. Tap the words To Do List. This brings up the list of available applications.

7. From the list, tap Calculator.

8. The Calculator icon is on the right side of the display. Tap the word Calc. This brings up the list of available applications.

9. From this list, tap To Do List.

10. Tap the Applications soft button (*Do not* touch Default!) This returns you to the Application Picker screen.

11. Now press the To Do hard button at the bottom of your Palm. The calculator should come on.

> **Don't Panic** If another application appeared, panic. You may have accidentally picked the wrong program. Repeat the process from step 2.

You have successfully reprogrammed the buttons. Great. But now you decide you prefer to return to the way it was. No problem. Here is what you do.

1. Repeat Steps 1-5 above.
2. Tap the Default button.
3. The settings should return to the default state.

See how easy it is!

Pen Setting

You may recall that in Lesson 4 I told you about a way to bring up the keyboard by moving the stylus (pen) from the Graffiti Pad to the top of the main display screen. I called this a special tap sequence. In the Button Preferences section, it is called a Pen preference. To set the Pen preference, tap Pen at the bottom of the main Buttons Preferences screen (see Figure 5.8). You will then see the Pen Preference screen (see Figure 5.10).

To set the Pen preference, follow these steps:

1. Tap Pen at the bottom of the main Buttons Preferences screen (refer to Figure 5.8). You will then see the Pen Preference screen (see Figure 5.10).
2. Tap the existing preference to view the complete list of choices (see Figure 5.11).

    - Backlight
    - Keyboard
    - Graffiti Help
    - Turn Off & Lock
    - Beam Data

FIGURE 5.10   Pen Preference screen.

FIGURE 5.11   Complete list of Pen preferences.

3. Tap the new preference.
4. Tap OK to accept or Cancel to return to the Main Buttons Preferences screen.

HotSync

You can customize the button located on the Palm HotSync cradle, and set the option modem for the PalmIII.

> **HotSync** HotSync is the name of the Palm program that enables you to synchronize (or copy) the data stored in your Palm with your PC and vice versa. This means that once copied, should the data on your Palm be lost, you can quickly restore from your PC.

If you wish to change these preferences, follow these steps:

1. Tap HotSync at the bottom of the main Buttons Preferences screen. You are now looking at the HotSync Buttons main screen.

2. To change the setting for the cradle, tap the existing selection located next to the cradle icon. This displays a list of available applications. (see Figure 5.12).

3. Tap on the application you choose as your new preference.

FIGURE 5.12   Application list.

4. Repeat this procedure for the Palm III modem.

5. Tap OK to accept or Cancel to return to the main Buttons Preferences screen.

PALM APPLICATIONS, PREFERENCES, DIGITIZER

The Digitizer is designed to align the screen for data entry. If you had to perform a hard reset (see Lesson 2), you would need to set the Digitizer.

> **Screen Alignment** Because the Palm requires you to tap the screen to enter data, the unit must understand your "touch" in order to move around the screen properly. When you align the screen, these settings help the Palm understand your movements.

To set the Digitizer, follow these steps:

1. Go to the category list, located in the upper-right corner of the main display (see Figure 5.13).

2. Tap the list to view the full list.

3. Tap Digitizer. You are now looking at the Digitizer alignment.

FIGURE 5.13   Category list.

4. Tap the screen as instructed. The screen then returns to the last Preferences menu you were using.

PALM APPLICATIONS, PREFERENCES, FORMATS

The Palm OS enables you to store format preferences.

> **Formats** Formats are the manner in which specific types of data (time or numbers, for example) are displayed. If your company forms or reports require you to meet a particular standard, you will want to be sure your formats are set to meet that standard.

The formats you can store include the following:

- Preset to (Country)
- Time
- Date
- Week Starts
- Numbers

Let's briefly review each format.

PRESET TO (COUNTRY)

The Palm contains a list of many countries for which the other information is preloaded (see Figure 5.14). To view this list, tap the default country on the screen. If you wish to use a different country, select that country from the list by tapping on it. You will see the defaults for the other settings change automatically.

54　LESSON 5

Figure 5.14　Preloaded country list.

TIME

To view this list, follow these steps:

1. Tap the default time format on the screen.

2. If you wish to use a different time format, select that format from the list by tapping on it.

DATE

To view this list, follow these steps:

1. Tap the default date format on the screen.

2. If you wish to use a different date format, select that format from the list by tapping on it.

WEEK STARTS

To view this list, follow these steps:

1. Tap the default day on the screen.

2. If you wish to use a different day, select that day from the list by tapping on it.

NUMBERS

To view this list, follow these steps:

1. Tap the default number format on the screen.

2. If you wish to use a different number format, select that format from the list by tapping on it.

PALM APPLICATIONS, PREFERENCES, MODEM

Your Palm does not have a built-in modem. You may elect to purchase an optional modem from Palm or a third-party vendor. If you plan to use a modem with your Palm, you will set the modem preferences here. The preferences include the following:

- Modem (manufacturer)
- Speed
- Speaker
- Flow Ctl (Flow Control)
- String
- Touchtone or Rotary

> **Modems** Modem stands for modulate/demodulate. A modem is the device that enables your computer, or in this case, your Palm computer, to access a computer, the Internet or other computer network and communicate data back and forth.

> **Know Your Modem** Make certain to consult the documentation that comes with your modem before setting the preferences.

Let's briefly review each of these.

MODEM (MANUFACTURER)

The Palm contains a list of many modem vendors for which the other information is preloaded (see Figure 5.15). To view this list, tap the default modem on the screen. If you wish to use a different modem, select that modem from the list by tapping on it. You will see the defaults for the other settings change automatically.

FIGURE 5.15 Preloaded Modem Vendor list

SPEED

This is the speed at which the modem will communicate—normally 57600bps. To view this list, follow these steps:

1. Tap the default speed on the screen.
2. If you wish to use a different modem speed, select that speed from the list by tapping on it.

Speaker

The speaker control sets the level at which you will hear noise coming through the speaker during communications. Your choices are Off, High, Medium, or Low. To view this list, tap the default level on the screen. If you wish to use a different level, select that speed from the list by tapping on it.

> **Keeping the Audio On** You may wish to keep the speaker on at least low so that you can verify the modem actually dials and makes a connection.

Flow Ctl (Flow Control)

This is how modems communicate with one another. Your choices are standard, On (also called XON) or Off (also called XOFF). To view this list, tap the default setting on the screen. If you wish to use a different setting, select that setting from the list by tapping on it.

> **Flow Control** Flow Control is the manner in which modems communicate. When modems talk to each other, they send requests back and fourth asking whether it is okay to send more data along the phone line. If the answer is no, the sending modem must wait until the receiving modem says that it is okay to send. Your modem documentation should explain this in more detail.

String

Modems send a "set up string" before they begin dialing. The default string for the modem you selected will be on the screen. You can edit this string using normal data entry procedures. You will need to change this only in rare circumstances, primarily only when instructed to do so.

> **Not Sure?** If you are not sure about your set up string, consult your modem documentation or system administrator.

Touchtone or Rotary

Select the appropriate one for the type of telephone line you are using—normally Touchtone.

> Although most phones are now touchtone, you should confirm this with your phone system's administrator or local phone company.

Palm Applications, Preferences, Network

If you plan to use your Palm computer to connect with the Internet, you can set the preferences here. You can store information about the Internet service provider (ISP) or other computer network you may call with your modem. After you store this information, you can dial automatically instead of having to enter it each time.

You can store the following basic information:

- Service
- Username
- Password
- Phone number

Let's briefly review each of these.

SERVICE

This refers to the name of your ISP. The Palm has a default list, or you can enter your own. To view the default list, tap the word Service on the screen. If you wish to use a different setting, select that setting from the list by tapping on it. If you wish to enter another name, you can do so by following normal data entry procedures.

USERNAME

Enter your username for your ISP.

PASSWORD

Enter your password.

> **Filing Your Password** If you don't enter a password, you will receive a prompt for one during the logon process.

> **Security Alert 1** Once entered, the Palm is designed so that it will *not* display your network password. If it prompts you for the password during a dial up session, however, the password will appear onscreen as you enter it. Be sure that no one is looking over your shoulder.

> **Security Alert 2** Once entered, your network password can't be deleted unless you perform a hard reset. That means if you don't also use a Palm password and lock you Palm, someone could get access to your Internet connection or company computer. Think carefully before entering your network password here.

PHONE NUMBER

To enter the phone number for your ISP, follow these steps:

1. Tap on the Tap to enter phone box. You will then see the Phone Number entry screen (see Figure 5.16)

FIGURE 5.16   Phone Setup screen.

2. **Phone #**. At this point, you can enter the phone number. Enter the phone number using normal data entry procedures.

3. **Dial prefix**. Use this to indicate numbers to be dialed prior to dialing the actual phone number. Many businesses require that you to dial 9 to get an outside line, for example. Using a comma after the 9 pauses the dialing sequence, to give the phone system a chance to provide the outside line. Remember to enable the check box if you need this feature.

4. **Disable call waiting**. Next, you will want to disable call waiting. If you are calling from a telephone equipped with call waiting, you should disable the call waiting prior to making a modem call. Otherwise, the call-waiting tone could disconnect your modem call.

5. **Use calling card**. You may wish to enter your calling card number here if you will be making calling card calls. Remember to enable the check box if you need this feature.

6. After you have completed entering the data, tap OK or Cancel to return to the main Network Preferences screen.

> **Commas Are Important**   Remember to use commas to indicate a pause, for example, between disable call waiting and the phone number.

DETAILS (NETWORK)

At the bottom of the main Network Preferences screen, you have the option to select Details. Tap this to go to the Details screen (see Figure 5.17).

FIGURE 5.17   Details screen.

You can enter additional technical network details for the ISP or computer you are dialing in to. If you are unsure of this information, please check with your ISP or system administrator prior to changing any settings.

Palm Applications, Preferences, Owner

The Preferences application has a section where you can enter information about the owner of the Palm. If you set a password and then turn off and lock your Palm, this information appears when the unit is turned back on.

To add owner information, follow these steps:

1. Go to the category list, located in the upper-right corner of the main display (see Figure 5.18).

FIGURE 5.18   Category list.

2. Tap the list to view the full list (see Figure 5.19).

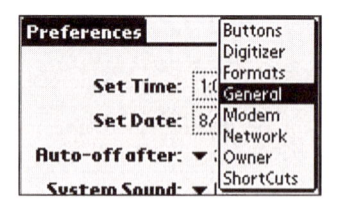

FIGURE 5.19   Full category list.

3. Tap Owner. You are now looking at the main Owner information screen (see Figure 5.20).

MAXIMIZING YOUR PALM—PREFERENCES AND APPLICATIONS   63

FIGURE 5.20   Main Owner information screen.

4. Add your name, address, telephone number, and other information here. This could be used as a form of identification if you should lose your Palm.

PALM APPLICATIONS, PREFERENCES, SHORTCUTS

Your Palm OS can store shortcuts to help you save keystrokes.

To view the list of available shortcuts, follow these steps:

1. Go to the category list, located in the upper-right corner of the main display (see Figure 5.21).

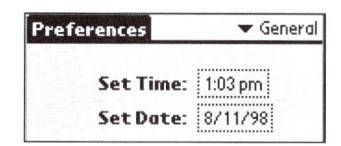

FIGURE 5.21   Category list.

2. Tap the list to view the full list (see Figure 5.22).

64 Lesson 5

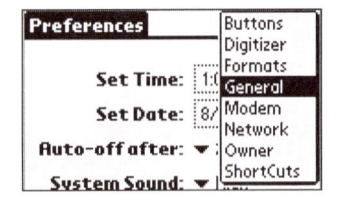

FIGURE 5.22 Full category list.

3. Tap ShortCuts. You are now looking at the main ShortCuts Preferences screen (see Figure 5.23).

FIGURE 5.23 Main Shortcut Preferences screen.

Add a New Shortcut

To add a new shortcut to the list, follow these steps (these steps follow the preceding three steps):

4. Tap New at the bottom of the screen. The Shortcut Entry screen appears (see Figure 5.24).

FIGURE 5.24 ShortCut Entry screen.

5. Type in the shortcut name and shortcut text where indicated.

6. When you are done, tap OK. To cancel the entry, tap Cancel.

> **Entering a Space** You may wish to enter a space at the end of the shortcut text so that you can continue typing in a normal manner after using the shortcut.

EDIT AN EXISTING SHORTCUT

To edit an existing shortcut, follow these steps:

1. Tap Edit at the bottom of the screen. The ShortCut Edit screen appears (see Figure 5.25).

FIGURE 5.25   ShortCut Edit screen.

2. Edit the shortcut as required.

3. When you are done, tap OK. To cancel the entry, tap Cancel.

DELETE A SHORTCUT

To delete an existing shortcut, tap Delete at the bottom of the screen. You will then be asked to confirm the deletion.

USING SHORTCUTS

Using Shortcuts during the normal data entry process is very easy. A simple Graffiti stroke activates the entire thing.

Just follow these steps:

1. Go to your application (for example, Memo Pad).

2. Go to the point in the application at which you wish to use the shortcut.

3. Enter the ShortCut Graffiti stroke (see Figure 5.26).

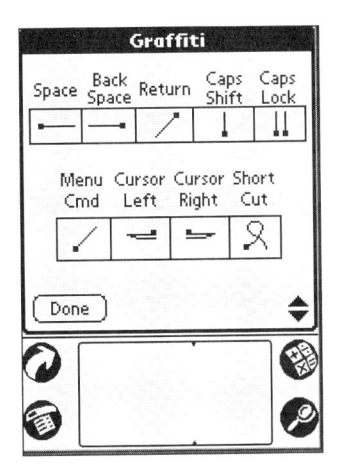

Maximizing Your Palm—Preferences and Applications 67

FIGURE 5.26 Shortcut Graffiti stroke.

4. Enter the shortcut characters that activate the shortcut.
5. The predefined shortcut text appears automatically.
6. If you wish to delete this text, enter Backspace Graffiti strokes.

In this lesson, you learned how to set the date and time, day and time formats and how to reprogram the Application buttons in your Palm. In the next lesson, you start to use applications. First up is the Address Book.

LESSON 6

APPLICATIONS—ADDRESS BOOK

In this lesson, you learn how to add and search for entries in your Address Book.

USING THE ADDRESS BOOK

Storing address information is one of the most common uses of the Palm. Just think, you longer have to carry around a paper address book. No more having to write new names by hand, only to have to transfer them later to a new address book. No more Rolodex at your desk—you can simply sync your Palm to your desktop and have an online and a portable version.

Let's take a look at the Address Book. To get to the Address Book, follow these steps:

1. Turn on the Palm.
2. Tap the Applications soft button.
3. From the main screen (or Applications menu), tap the Address icon (see Figure 6.1).

FIGURE 6.1 The Address Book icon.

You are now looking at the main Address Book screen (see Figure 6.2).

FIGURE 6.2   The main Address Book screen.

ADDING A NEW ENTRY

Adding new names to your Address Book is easy. To enter a new name, follow these steps:

1. Tap New. This takes you to the main Address Book data entry screen (see Figure 6.3). I suggest you make at least one sample entry.

2. Enter the appropriate information on each line shown:

    - Last name
    - First name
    - Title
    - Company
    - Work (telephone number)
    - Home (telephone number)
    - Fax
    - Other

- E-mail
- Address

FIGURE 6.3 The main Address Book data entry screen

3. For the telephone-related categories, you can choose each field from a list. To see the list, tap on the default that has a down arrow next to it. The list of available categories will appear. To choose a different category, tap that category.

- Address
- City
- State
- Country
- Custom 1
- Custom 2
- Custom 3
- Custom 4

4. After you have completed entering the data, tap Done to store it in your Address Book.

> **Collect Business Cards? Use a Scanner!** If you plan to enter larger amounts of address information from business cards, consider the purchase of a business card scanner. Several vendors offer scanner software that enters the scanned data automatically entered directly in the Palm Desktop software, which then can be hotsynced to your Palm.

ADDING DETAILS

You can add additional details to your entry at this point. To do so, tap Details. You will see the Address Entry Details screen (see Figure 6.4).

FIGURE 6.4 Address Entry Details screen.

- Show in List

    Decide which phone number you want to show in the main address book list.

- Category

Decide which category you want the entry listed in. Categories are covered in more detail later in this lesson

- Private

    Mark the entry private. Private entries require a password to gain access.

Adding a Note

You can add a note to each entry containing additional information about this person. You might include the names of the person's spouse and children. You might have other information that could be useful in the future, such as the college he or she attended.

To add a note, tap Note. This brings you to the Note entry screen (see Figure 6.5). After you have filled in the information, tap Done.

Figure 6.5 Note entry screen.

Viewing an Existing Entry

Viewing an existing entry is easy. To try it, make a sample entry following the preceding steps. Then follow these steps:

1. Go to the main Address Book screen.

2. You should now see an abbreviated list of entries, starting with last name and including a phone number. This list should include the sample entry you just made.

3. To view the entire entry, just tap on that entry. All the information you entered previously should now be displayed. If the information takes up more than one screen, use the up/down arrows at the bottom of the screen to move as needed.

4. When you are done, tap Done.

5. To edit this entry, tap Edit.

6. To add a new entry to your Address Book, tap New.

LOCATING AN EXISTING ENTRY

So now you have entered quite a few names in the Address Book. So many, in fact, that it takes too long to scroll up and down to find a particular one. No problem. Address Book has a Look Up feature.

1. Go to the main Address Book screen. At the bottom of the screen, you see the words **Look Up** and a field to enter data.

2. Begin to enter the last name of the person you are looking for. The program will automatically move to the nearest entry with that name.

USING CATEGORIES

As your Address Book gets larger, another way to ease your search is to use categories. Categories enable you to create segments, which can be displayed on request. Let me explain.

Let's say you have several hundred entries in your Address Book. If you think about it, most of these entries will fit into one primary category (for example, personal or business). Using categories can make it easier to view your Address Book and locate specific entries.

Assigning a Category

To assign a category to a specific entry, you select it from a default list. Follow these steps:

1. Go to the main Address Book screen.

2. You should now see an abbreviated list of entries, starting with last name and including a phone number. This list should include the sample entry you made earlier.

3. To view the entire entry, just tap on that entry. All the information you entered previously should now be displayed. The category this entry is presently assigned to is displayed in the upper-right corner(see Figure 6.6).

Figure 6.6   Sample address entry.

4. If you wish to assign a different category, tap Edit. This brings up the Address Edit screen (see Figure 6.7).

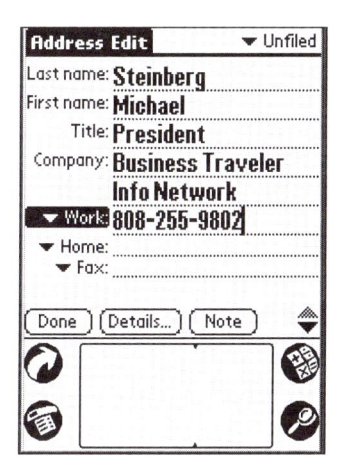

FIGURE 6.7   Sample Address Edit screen.

5. A down arrow now appears next to the assigned category name in the upper-right corner. Tap that name.

6. You can now see the list of available categories (see Figure 6.8). To change the category for this entry, tap the new category. The pull-down list will close, and the new category name will appear.

FIGURE 6.8   Categories list

7. If you have completed editing the entry, tap Done.

EDITING OR ADDING CATEGORIES

To edit or add categories, follow these steps:

1. To edit or add categories, follow steps 1–5 from the preceding list. When you see the list of available categories, tap Edit Categories. You will see the Edit Categories screen (see Figure 6.9).

Figure 6.9   Edit Categories screen.

2. To add a new category, tap New. This brings up the Edit Categories name screen (see Figure 6.10).

FIGURE 6.10   Edit Categories name screen

3. Enter the new category name and tap OK.
4. To exit without changes, tap Cancel.

To rename an existing category, follow these steps:

1. Follow steps 1–5 in the assigning-a-category list.
2. Select that category by tapping on it.
3. Then tap Rename. This brings up the Edit Categories name screen (see Figure 6.11).

FIGURE 6.11   Edit Categories name screen.

  4. Enter the new category name and tap OK.
  5. To exit without changes, tap Cancel.

To delete an existing category, follow these steps:

  1. Follow the preceding steps 1–5.
  2. Select the category by tapping on it.
  3. Tap Delete.
  4. You are prompted to confirm before the category is deleted.

> **Deleting!**   If you delete a category in use, all entries previously using that category will then be listed as **Unfiled**. You may wish to locate and recategorize these entries prior to deleting the category.

Menu Commands

The Address Book has three classes of pull-down menu commands: Record, Edit, and Options. To bring up the pull-down menu bar, tap the Menu icon. The next sections discuss each command.

Menu Commands—Record

These are commands you can perform on a record or group of records (see Figure 6.12). They specifically apply to the infrared beam.

Figure 6.12   Menu Commands—Record.

Beam Category

1. Select the category you wish to send to another Palm user.
2. Tap Beam Category.
3. All the records in that category will be sent to that user's Address Book.

Beam Business Card

1. Select the business card record you wish to send to another Palm user.
2. Tap Beam Business Card.
3. Your information will then appear in the other Palm's Address Book.

Menu Commands—Edit

Lesson 14 covers the Edit menu commands.

Menu Commands—Options

These are system options you can change that will apply only to the Address Book program (see Figure 6.13). These include the font and how information is displayed.

FIGURE 6.13   Menu Commands—Options.

Font
Select the font you wish from the list shown.

Preferences
Use this to tell the program whether you want to remember the last category used and to tell the program the order in which you want the names displayed (see Figure 6.14).

APPLICATIONS—ADDRESS BOOK   81

FIGURE 6.14   Menu commands, Options, Preferences menu.

- Remember last category

    The system will display *all* unless you tell it otherwise.

- List By

    Choose from the list provided if you wish to view the list in another manner.

- Rename Custom Fields

    Use this command to place a new name in any of the custom fields. Keep in mind that this changes the Address Book itself, not just the individual record.

ABOUT ADDRESS BOOK

This tells you the version number of the program. Tap OK to exit.

In this lesson, you learned how to use the Address Book. In the next lesson, you learn about the Date Book.

Lesson 7

Applications— Date Book

In this lesson, you learn how to use and customize the Date Book.

Date Book

What is the Date Book?

The Date Book is designed to track your daily activities, both personal and business. It keeps your list of meetings and other events, along with personal information such as birthday reminders.

Because many people purchase a Palm to replace their Filofax, Day Runner, or other day planners, the Date Book is a very popular Palm application. The Date Book program enables you to easily enter new event information, as well as quickly view existing event and general calendar information. It's a great tool.

> **Remember: HotSync!** Date Book and Address Book are the two most popular applications. They contain data that is vital for daily operation. Remember to hotsync (covered in Lesson 20) on a regular basis so that a copy of this information also resides on your PC.

To open the Date Book, follow these steps:

1. You can push the Date Book hard application button located on the lower left side of the Palm.

Or…

1. Turn on the Palm.
2. Tap the Applications soft button to bring up the main Applications menu (if this menu is not already onscreen).
3. Tap the Date Book icon (see Figure 7.1). This brings you to the main Date Book screen for today's date (see Figure 7.2).

FIGURE 7.1 The Date Book icon.

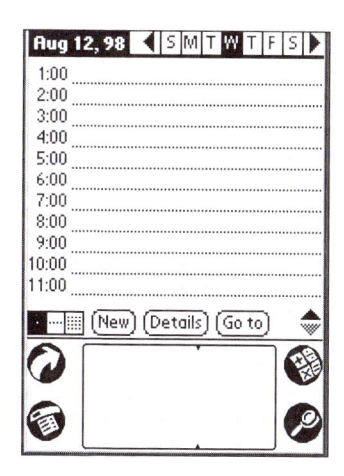

FIGURE 7.2 The main Date Book screen.

> **It's That Time Again** You can see what time it is by tapping the date located in the upper-left corner of the display.

VIEWING A SPECIFIC DATE

To view another date, you have several options:

- Select another day of the week from main screen, or

LESSON 7

- Select a date one week before or after today's date, or
- Use the Go to option

To view another day of that week, use the day of week indicator at the top of the display. Choose the day of the week you wish to view by tapping on the letter associated with that day.

To view the date one week before or after today's date, follow these steps:

1. Tap Go To. This will take you to a screen that will allow you to enter a new date (see Figure 7.3)

FIGURE 7.3 The Go to Date screen.

2. To select the year, use the right/left arrows located on each side of the year displayed at the top of then screen, until the correct year appears.

3. To select the month, tap the correct month from the list that appears below the year indicator.

4. To select the day, tap the correct day from the list displayed below the month list.

5. When you select the day, the application will automatically return to the main Date Book screen and display the activity for that date.

APPLICATIONS—DATE BOOK   85

6. To cancel you entry without changes, tap Cancel. To return to today's date, tap Today.

ADDING A NEW ENTRY

To add a new entry, follow these steps:

1. Go to the date on which you want the new entry to appear, using the instructions outlined previously.
2. Tap New.

Or...

Tap the time you wish the event to start on the main display.

Or...

Enter the Start time hour using Graffiti.

3. You will then see the Set Time screen (see Figure 7.4).

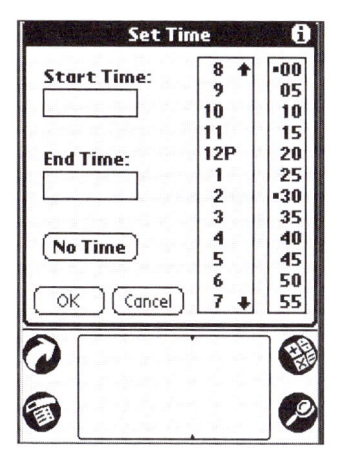

FIGURE 7.4   Set Time entry screen

4. To set the start time, tap the time box below Start Time.
5. Tap the hour and minutes from the list located at the right side of the screen. If the hour you need is not on the screen, use the

up/down arrows provided to move the list until the hour you need appears.

6. The End Time will automatically change to one hour later than the start time. To set a different end time, tap the time box below End Time and follow the same procedure as previously outlined.

7. After the start and end time are acceptable, tap OK.

8. To exit without changes, tap Cancel. This returns you to the main calendar screen for that day.

9. To enter a reminder or event that does not require a time (such as birthday or anniversary) tap No Time.

> **Location, Location, Location** If you tap No Time, the event will appear at the top of that day's calendar with a diamond symbol next to it.

VIEWING EVENT DETAILS

For every event in your Date Book, you can specify the following details:

- *Alarm.* To notify you of an appointment
- *Repeat.* To repeat the appointment automatically from week to week or month to month
- *Private.* To keep the appointment hidden from view

While viewing or modifying this information, you can also change the time or date of the event.

To view the details of an entry, follow these steps:

1. You must first go to the date and time of that entry, using the instructions outlined previously.

2. Tap Details. This brings up the Event Details screen (see Figure 7.5).

APPLICATIONS—DATE BOOK   87

FIGURE 7.5   Event Details screen.

Let's step through each item.

CHANGING APPOINTMENT TIME

If you wish to change the time of the event, tap the time shown. You then follow the procedure outlined previously for setting an event time.

CHANGING THE DATE

If you wish to change the date of the event, tap the date shown. You then follow the procedure outlined previously for setting an event date.

SETTING THE ALARM

You might wish to get an audible alarm to remind you of this event. To tell the system to sound an alarm at the start of this event, check the Alarm box. You may then specify at what time you want the alarm to occur prior to the event by first entering an amount (for example, 5), and then specifying the duration from the list provided (minutes, hours, or days).

LESSON 7

> **Oops!** My alarm didn't go off. Alarms are silent for untimed events.

REPEATING THE EVENT

If you wish to make the treat a repeating event, tap the box next to Repeat. This brings up the Change Repeat screen (see Figure 7.6). You then set the repeat option.

FIGURE 7.6 Change Repeat screen.

Your have the following options:

- None (default)

    This indicates that this is a one-time event.

- Day

    Use this to set a repeat for every x number of days. You can use this as a reminder for an event that occurs on a regular basis or to indicate an event such as a trip, that will have an end date. Specify this information in the fields provided.

- Week

    Use this for an event that will occur once every week or *x* weeks (for example, turning in a time sheet or taking out the trash). You can also specify an end on date and a repeat on day of the week. Specify this information in the fields provided.

- Month

    Use this for an event that will occur once every month or *x* months (for example, an organizational meeting). You can also specify and end on date and a repeat by day or date. Specify this information in the fields provided.

- Year

    Use this for an event that will occur once a year(for example, a birthday or anniversary). You can also specify how often (every 2, 3, 4…years) and an end on date if applicable. Specify this information in the fields provided.

- Private

    To mark this event private, check the Private box. This requires you to enter a password to view information on the event.

- Note

    If you wish to add additional details to this event, tap Note and enter the information.

After you have completed entering the details, tap OK. To cancel your entry without changes, tap Cancel. To delete the event completely, tap Delete.

> **Deleting Events** If you elect to delete the event at this point, you will *not* be asked for a confirmation. Don't use Delete unless you are sure.

ADDITIONAL VIEWING OPTIONS

If you look at the lower-left portion of the display, you will see three connected boxes: one with 1 dot, one with 4 dots, and one with 20 dots. You are not limited to viewing one day at a time. You can also view the present week or month or another week or month using these boxes. Here's what to do.

WEEK AT A GLANCE

To see the present week, follow these steps:

1. Tap the middle box with 4 dots. It brings up the one week summary screen (see Figure 7.7). This gives you some idea of the amount of activity for that week.

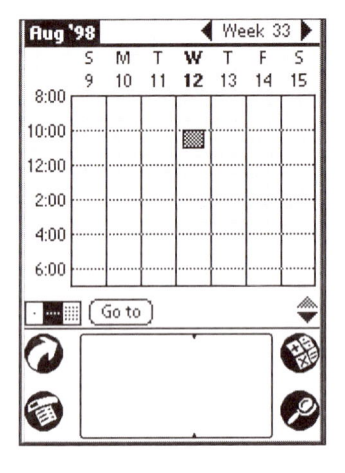

FIGURE 7.7 A one week summary screen.

2. From this screen, you can move forward or ahead one week, change to the daily or monthly view, jump to a specific event or day of the week, or go to any other date.

3. To move forward or ahead one week, tap the right or left arrow located by the week-number indicator at the top right of the display.

APPLICATIONS—DATE BOOK   91

To change to a monthly or daily view, tap the appropriate box in the lower-left side of the display. To jump to specific event or day, tap that event or day in the Week at a Glance section located in the middle of the display.

To move to another date, tap Go to .

VIEWING THE MONTH AT A GLANCE

To see the present month, follow these steps:

1. Tap the middle box with 20 dots. This brings up the one month summary screen (see Figure 7.8). This will give you some idea of the amount of activity for that month.

FIGURE 7.8   A one month summary screen.

2. From this screen, you can move forward or ahead one month, change to the daily or weekly view, jump to a specific event or day of the week, or go to any other date.

3. To move forward or ahead one month, tap the right or left arrow located at the top right of the display.

To change to a weekly or daily view, tap the appropriate box in the lower-left side of the display.

To jump to specific event or day, tap that event or day in the Month at a Glance section located in the middle of the display.

To move to another date, tap Go to.

Menu Commands

Menu commands are additional capabilities for a given application. To view the menu commands, tap the Menu soft button located at the lower-right section of your display, next to the Graffiti Pad. You have several menu commands available for the Date Book:

- Record
- Edit
- Options

Menu Commands—Record

There are Graffiti shortcuts that enable you move to or perform a command with two strokes (see Figure 7.9), including the following:

Figure 7.9 Menu commands—Record.

- New Event
- Delete Event
- Attach Note
- Delete Note
- Purge
- Beam Event

MENU COMMANDS—EDIT

Lesson 14 describes the Edit commands.

MENU COMMANDS—OPTIONS

These are system options you can change that will only apply to the Date Book program (see Figure 7.10). These include the font and how information is displayed.

FIGURE 7.10   Menu commands—Options.

Font

The Font option enables you to select the type of font. Tap your choice from the list shown. Tap OK to accept or tap Cancel to exit without changes

Preferences

From the main menu, you can also set preferences for this application only (see Figure 7.11).

FIGURE 7.11 Menu commands—Options—Preferences

You can set the following preferences from this menu:

- *Start Time.* Your preferred start of day.
- *End Time.* Your preferred end of day.

> **Times Are Changing** You can change the start/end time from this menu by using the up/down arrows located at the right of the time display.

- *Alarm Preset.* This enables you to set a default alarm for every activity. Tap the check box to enable and enter the amount of time in minutes before an event you would like the alarm to sound.

- *Alarm Sound.* Choose the type of sound from a list by tapping on the default sound shown.

- *Remind Me.* How many times do you want to be reminded by alarm? Choose the amount from the list by tapping on the default amount shown.

- *Play Every.* How often (in minutes) do you want the alarm to sound before it shuts off by itself? Choose the amount from the list by tapping on the default shown.

> **This news is very alarming!** Checking Alarm Preset sets an alarm for every event, including untimed events. Think carefully before enabling this feature.

DISPLAY OPTIONS

Display options enable you to decide what information appears in the Day and Month view (see Figure 7.12).

Figure 7.12 Menu commands—Options—Display options.

Under display options, you can choose several settings:

- *Day View*. Enables you to view your events by day.

- *Show Time Bars*. Disabling this feature removes the time bars from the main Date Book daily display.

> **Time Bar** The time bar indicates the duration of the event by placing a bar that connects the beginning and end times.

- *Compress Day View*. Disabling this feature requires the system to show all hours on the daily display.

> **Where Did the Time Go?** Enabling Compress Day View means the Date Book daily display is designed to show all your daily events within a single screen if possible. It may not display hours of inactivity during the day in order to get all the events on the one screen.

- *Month View: Show Timed Events.* Tells the system whether you want to show timed events on the display. Generally, you will want to keep this box checked.

- *Show Untimed Events.* Tells the system whether you want to show untimed events on the display. You need to decide whether you need untimed events shown.

> **Reduce Screen Clutter** If you have both a busy schedule and many untimed events, you may want to keep the Show Untimed Events box unchecked.

- *Show Daily Repeating Events.* Tells the system whether you want to show repeating events on the display.

Phone Look Up

This takes you directly to the main Address Book screen, so you can look up a name or phone number.

About Date Book

This tells you the version number of the program.

Tap OK to exit the display.

In this lesson, you learned how to enter events in the Date Book and how to check your calendar. In the next lesson, you learn to use the To Do List.

LESSON 8

APPLICATIONS— TO DO LIST

In this lesson, you learn how to create and use To Do lists.

TO DO LIST

What is the To Do List?

The average To Do List used to be a piece of paper containing your list of things you plan to do, people to meet, and places to go. The To Do List program doesn't just eliminate the paper, it takes these lists to the next level.

Using the Palm To Do List, you can not only track your completed tasks, but categorize them, check your history, and even create check lists that you can use on a recurring basis.

To open the To Do List program, follow these steps:

1. You can push the To Do hard application button located on the lower-right side of the Palm (see Figure 8.1).

   Or…

   Turn on the Palm.

   FIGURE 8.1   The To Do List icon.

2. Tap the *Applications* soft button to bring up the main Applications menu (if this menu is not already on screen).

3. Tap the To Do icon. This brings you to the main To Do List screen (see Figure 8.2).

FIGURE 8.2   Main To Do List screen.

Let's step through the basic functions—adding a new entry, viewing entry details, and changing the preferences.

ADDING A NEW ENTRY

To add a new To Do List entry, follow these steps:

1. Tap New. This adds a blank item to the To Do list. You can then enter a description of the item and add a note and assign a priority if applicable.

2. To assign a priority level, tap the default priority level shown. You will see a list of priority levels from 1–5 (see Figure 8.3).

FIGURE 8.3 Priority levels.

3. Tap the new priority level from this list.
4. To attach a note to this item, tap the Menu soft button.
5. From the Record pull-down menu, tap Attach Note (see Figure 8.4).

FIGURE 8.4 Attach Note.

APPLICATIONS—TO DO LIST   101

6. A note screen appears (see Figure 8.5). Fill in the note.

FIGURE 8.5   Note screen.

7. When the note is complete, tap Done.

8. If you wish to delete the note, tap Delete. You are asked to confirm before the note is deleted.

VIEWING DETAILS

To view details for a particular entry, you must first tap on a To Do list to select it. Then tap Details. The To Do Items Details screen appears (see Figure 8.6):

FIGURE 8.6 To Do item details.

You can then assign details to this item, as follows:

- Priority   Set the priority number from 1–5. This determines how the item appears on the list.

- Category   Choose a category from the list provided.

- Due Date   Choose a due date from the list provided.

- Private   To mark the to do item private, check the Private box. This requires you to enter a password to view the memo.

SHOW TO DO PREFERENCES

To view the To Do Preferences, tap Show from the main To Do List screen. The To Do Preferences screen appears (see Figure 8.7).

FIGURE 8.7   To Do Preferences.

You can then assign preferences as follows:

Sort by:

- Show Completed Items
- Show Only Due Items
- Record Completion Date
- Show Due Dates
- Show Priorities
- Show Categories

> **Preferred Display**   You can pick and choose your preferences here to meet your specific needs. You might only want to see due items to get an overview of what is due now. Later you might want to see due and completed items to see what percent of the work has been completed. You can switch back and forth whenever you want.

Menu Commands

Menu commands are additional capabilities for a given application—in this case, the To Do application. To view the menu commands, tap the Menu soft button located at the lower-right section of your display next to the Graffiti pad (see Figure 8.8). You have several Menu commands available for the To Do List.

FIGURE 8.8   The Menu icon.

Menu Commands—Record

These are commands you can perform on a record or group of records (see Figure 8.9).

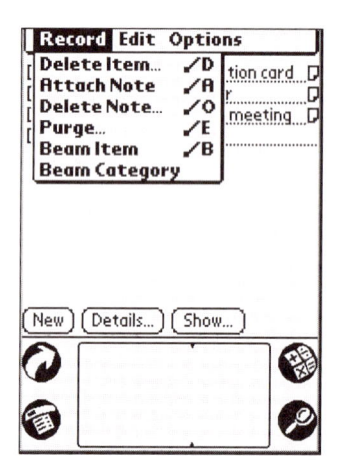

FIGURE 8.9   Menu commands—record.

- Delete Item   Delete the selected item.
- Attach Note   Bring up the Note Editor.

APPLICATIONS—TO DO LIST   105

- Delete Note   Delete the note attached to this item.
- Purge   Delete *all* To Do items marked completed.

> **Delete *All*?**   This is a command not to be used lightly. You might accidentally delete items you may want to use later.

- Beam Item   Transfer this item to another Palm.
- Beam Category   Transfer the entire category to another Palm.

> **Beam Me Up, Scotty?**   Whenever you transfer data, be sure you are sending the right information before you beam it over. Once you beam it, you can't beam it back.

MENU COMMANDS—EDIT

Lesson 14 covers these commands.

MENU COMMANDS—OPTION

These are system options you can change and other information that applies only to the To Do List program (see Figure 8.10). These include the font and how to look up phone information.

- Font   Select a different font size from the selections provided. Tap OK to accept. Tap Cancel to exit without saving changes.

```
Record Edit Options
□ 1 Send in  Font...        ✓F
□ 1 Send up  Phone Lookup   ✓L
□ 1 Plan ne: About To Do List
□ 1 Update web site
```

FIGURE 8.10   The Options menu.

- Phone Look Up   This takes you directly to the main Address Book screen, so you can look up a name or phone number. It also brings up the Phone Lookup screen (see Figure 8.11).

```
Phone Number Lookup:
Bressler, Suzanne   202-882-6397 W
Cohen, Arnold       809-769-2356 W
Cohen, Kenneth      801-546-7608 W
Fritz, Harrison     603-297-7390 H
Fritz, Olivia       972-870-4691 W
Goldman, Alex       212-653-9737 W
Isenberg, Steve     214-609-4529 H
McGruder, J.H.      808-340-9820 W
Steinberg, Graham   508-820-1997 W
Steinberg, Michael  808-255-9802 W
Summers, David      702-945-2700 W
Look Up: ........  (Add) (Cancel)
```

FIGURE 8.11   Phone Lookup screen.

- About To Do List   This tells you the version number of the program. Tap OK to exit.

> **Grocery List** Here is a very popular use for the To Do List. Create a category called Grocery. Then add the items that you buy at the grocery store on a regular basis (you know—coffee, milk, sugar, tissues, lima beans, whatever). Before your next trip, bring up the Grocery category and remove the items that you won't purchase by checking them complete. (Remember, you can always uncheck them later.) Then add any special-purchase items. You could even add notes to certain items to specify manufacturer and size. You then have a ready-made shopping list. As you go through the market, check each item as you pick it up. Great idea, eh?

> **Packing List** Are you a frequent traveler? Create a category called PackList and keep a list of your travel items (shirts, socks, suits, shoes, razor, toothbrush, and so on). Then you can check off each item before you leave home and before you check out of the hotel!

In this lesson, you learned how to use the To Do List program. In the next lesson, you learn to use the Memo Pad.

Lesson 9

Applications— Memo Pad

In this chapter, you learn how to write and view memos using the Memo Pad application on your Palm computer.

Using the Memo Pad

What is the Memo Pad?

The Memo Pad is a very basic word processor, perfect for jotting down quick notes, instructions, or other useful information.

The Memo Pad can hold all that information that would otherwise take up space in your wallet or briefcase. Many travelers keep their frequent traveler numbers in a Memo Pad entry, for example, instead of carrying around all those cards. You can use it to store driving directions, brief meeting notes, travel itineraries, or ideas for an upcoming project. I used it at a trade show to keep a list of booths I planned to visit instead of carrying the trade show guide.

To open the Memo Pad, follow these steps:

1. You can tap the Memo Pad hard application button located on the lower-right side of the Palm (see Figure 9.1).

FIGURE 9.1   The Memo Pad Icon.

Or...

Turn on the Palm.

2. Tap the Applications soft button to bring up the main Applications menu (if this menu is not already on screen).

3. Tap the Memo Pad icon. This brings you to the main Memo Pad screen (see Figure 9.2).

FIGURE 9.2 Main Memo Pad screen.

Let's step through the basic functions: adding a new entry, viewing an existing entry, and viewing memo details.

ADDING A NEW ENTRY

To add a new Memo Pad entry, follow these steps:

1. Tap New. This brings you to the new entry screen (see Figure 9.3).

2. Enter your memo.

3. After you have completed the memo, tap Done.

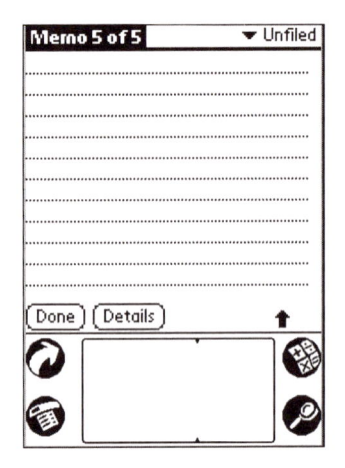

FIGURE 9.3 New Memo Edit screen.

VIEWING AN EXISTING ENTRY

To view an exiting entry, tap that entry. The entire memo will appear on screen.

> **Long Memos** If your memo is longer than one screen, you can move up and down the page either by using the Page Up/Down buttons located at the bottom of the Palm between the hard application buttons or by using the soft slide control located on the right side of the main display. Position your Stylus on the slide control and move up and down.

VIEWING MEMO DETAILS

Prior to completion, if you need to change or add a new category or mark the message private, tap Details. This brings up the Memo Details screen (see Figure 9.4). You can then specify the category and indicate whether you wish to mark the memo Private.

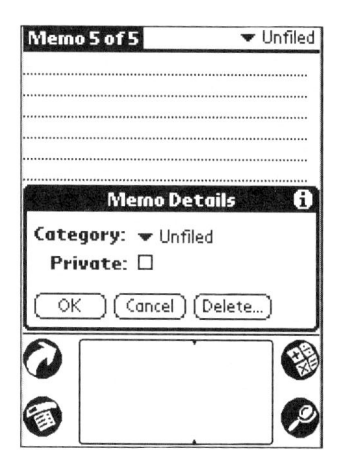

FIGURE 9.4 Memo Details screen.

CATEGORY

This is your opportunity to categorize the memo to make it easier to locate and view. If the memo is associated with a trip, for example, you might want to create a category that uses the destination. If the memo is associated with a particular event, such as a trade show, you might give the category the name of the show.

The system comes with a short sample list of categories. Tap the default category shown and tap Edit Categories to view the list of catergories currently showing (see Figure 9.5).

FIGURE 9.5 Edit Categories screen.

ENTERING A NEW CATEGORY

To enter a new category, follow these steps:

1. Tap the default category shown.

2. To add a new category, tap Edit Categories from that list. The Edit Categories screen appears.

3. View the list of categories currently showing.

4. Tap New. The new category entry screen appears (see Figure 9.6).

5. Enter the new category name and tap OK. The category has been added to your list.

APPLICATION—MEMO PAD   113

FIGURE 9.6   New category entry screen.

RENAMING A CATEGORY

If you would like to rename an existing category, follow these steps:

1. Tap the default category shown.

2. To add a new category, tap Edit Categories from that list. The Edit Categories screen appears.

3. View the list of categories currently showing.

4. Tap that category to select it.

5. Tap Rename. The new category entry screen appears (see Figure 9.7).

6. Enter the new category name and tap OK. This renamed category has now been added to your list.

FIGURE 9.7 New category entry screen.

DELETING A CATEGORY

If you want to delete a category, follow these steps:

1. Tap the default category shown.
2. Tap Edit Categories to bring up the Edit Categories screen.
3. View the list of categories currently showing.
4. Tap that category to select it.
5. Tap Delete and the category will be deleted from the list.

> **Automatic Deletion** If you select Delete the system will not ask you to confirm before deleting the name from the system. Be very sure you want to delete the name before you tap the Delete button.

After you have completed editing categories, tap OK This brings you back to the Memo Pad screen.

PRIVATE

To mark the memo as private, check the Private box. A password is required to view a private memo.

MENU COMMANDS

Menu commands are additional capabilities for a given application. To view the Menu commands, tap the Menu soft button located at the lower-right section of your display, next to the Graffiti pad (see Figure 9.8). You have several Menu commands available for the Memo Pad.

FIGURE 9.8   The Menu icon.

MENU COMMANDS—RECORD

These are system options you can change and other information that applies only to the Memo Pad program (see Figure 9.9). They are as follows:

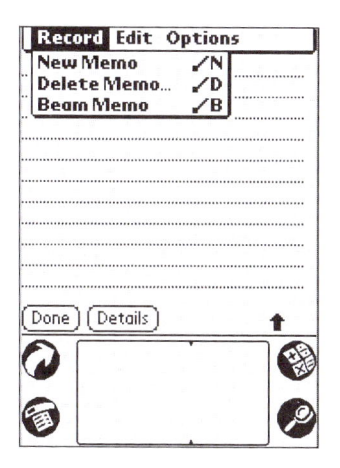

FIGURE 9.9   Menu commands—Record.

- New Memo   Opens a new memo.

- Delete Memo   Deletes the selected memo. You must confirm before the memo is deleted.

- Beam Memo   Beams selected memo to another Palm equipped with infrared.

Menu Commands—Edit

Lesson 14 covers these commands.

Menu Commands—Options

These are system options you can change and other information that applies only to the Memo Pad program (see Figure 9.10). These include the changing the font and looking up information from the Memo Pad.

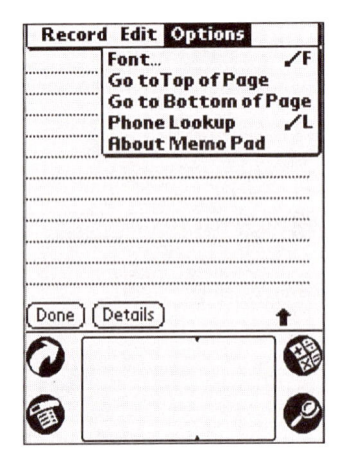

Figure 9.10   Menu commands—options.

Font

To change the font, select a different font size from the selections provided (see Figure 9.11). Tap OK to accept. Tap Cancel to exit without saving changes.

FIGURE 9.11 Font control screen.

The other options include:

- Go to Top of Page   Moves cursor to the top of the page.
- Go to Bottom of Page   Moves cursor to the bottom of the page.
- Phone Lookup   This takes you directly to the Main Address Book screen, where you can look up a name or phone number.
- About Memo Pad   This tells you the version number of the program. Tap OK to exit.

> **Frequent Traveler**   If you are a road warrior, here's a great use of the Memo Pad. Use an entry to store frequent traveler information such as travel-club membership numbers and airline reservation phone numbers.

In this lesson, you learned to use the Memo Pad. In the next lesson, you enter and track expenses into your Palm.

Lesson 10

Applications— Expense

In this lesson, you learn how to enter expenses into your Palm.

Expense

What is the Expense application?

The Expense program is for entering expenses incurred on a daily basis. Although the program was designed with business in mind, you can also use it for tracking personal or other expenses as well.

Expense is great for the business traveler. Next time you collect all those travel receipts, you can quickly enter them into this handy program and have your summary ready before you return home. This can save you time and headaches in preparing those expense reports. Hence the name Expense.

To open Expense, follow these steps:

1. Turn on the Palm.

2. Tap the Applications soft button to bring up the main Applications menu (if the menu is not already onscreen).

3. Tap the Expense icon (see Figure 10.1). This brings you to the main Expense screen (see Figure 10.2).

Figure 10.1 The Expense icon.

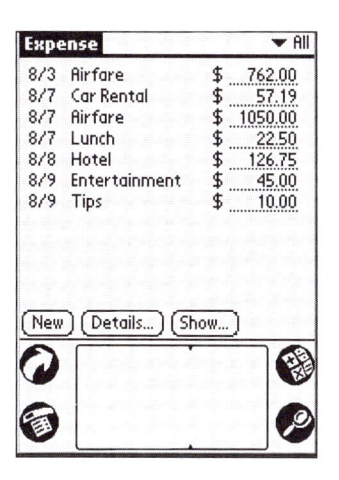

FIGURE 10.2 Main Expense screen.

Let's step through the basic functions—add a new entry, view receipt details, and add a note to an entry.

ADDING A NEW ENTRY

To make a new entry, tap New. A new entry appears on the display (see Figure 10.3).

FIGURE 10.3 New Expense entry.

CHANGE DATE

To change the date of an expense, follow these steps:

1. Tap the date shown. This brings you to the Date page, where you can choose a new date (see Figure 10.4).

FIGURE 10.4 Date screen.

2. If the current settings are correct, tap Today. The application will automatically return to the main Expense screen.

3. To select the year, use the right/left arrows located on each side of the year displayed at the top of the screen until the correct year appears.

4. To select the month, tap the correct month from the list that appears below the year indicator.

5. To select the day, tap the correct day from the list below the month list.

6. When you select the day, the application will automatically return to the main Expense screen.

7. If at any time you wish to end the entry without changes, tap Cancel. The application will automatically return to the main Expense screen.

EXPENSE TYPE

To select the type of expense, tap Expense Type. This brings up a list of expense types stored in the system. Move up or down on the list using the Up/Down arrows located at the bottom and top of the list display. Select the applicable type by tapping on it.

> **It Just Makes Cents!** The system automatically adds two decimal places to the amount. Adding a decimal place manually can cause problems.

EXPENSE AMOUNT

After you have selected the type of expense, enter the amount of the expense in the field shown.

VIEWING RECEIPT DETAILS

After you make an entry, you can add additional details by tapping Details. You will then see the Expense Details screen (see Figure 10.5).

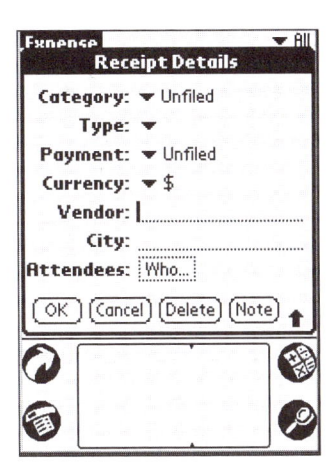

FIGURE 10.5 Expense Details screen.

Lesson 10

Let's step through each detailed item.

CATEGORY

This is your opportunity to categorize the expense to make it easier to locate and view. If the expense is associated with a trip, for example, you might want to create a category that uses the destination. If the expenses were associated with a particular event, such as a trade show, you might give the category the name of the show.

Expense comes with a short sample list of categories. Tap the default category shown and tap Edit Categories to view the list (see Figure 10.6).

FIGURE 10.6 Edit Categories screen.

ADDING A NEW ENTRY

To enter a new category, follow these steps:

1. Tap New. Ten new category entry screen appears (see Figure 10.7).
2. Enter the new category name.
3. Tap the OK button. This category has now been added to your list.

FIGURE 10.7 New category entry screen.

RENAMING A CATEGORY

To rename an existing category, follow these steps:

1. Tap a category to select it.
2. Tap Rename. The new category entry screen appears (see Figure 10.8).
3. Enter the new category name.
4. Tap the OK button. The category has now been renamed on your list.

FIGURE 10.8 New category entry screen.

DELETING A CATEGORY

To delete a category, follow these steps:

1. Tap a category to select it.

2. Tap Delete. The category will be deleted from the list.

> **Automatic Deletion** If you select Delete, the system will not ask you to confirm before deleting the name from the system. Be very sure you want to delete the name before you tap the Delete button.

3. After you have completed editing categories, tap OK. You return to the Expense Details screen.

TYPE

To change the type of expense, follow these steps:

1. Tap the default type shown. This brings up a list of expense types stored in the system (see Figure 10.9).

APPLICATIONS—EXPENSE 125

FIGURE 10.9   Expense category list.

2. Move up or down on the list using the Up/Down arrows located at the bottom and top of the list display.

3. Select the applicable type by tapping on it.

You will note that most of the expense categories are for business travel. Be sure to review your company travel policy or check with your accountant on how best to track and enter your travel expenses. In addition, if you use a standard set of categories, you can quickly find all entries in that category using the Find application (see Lesson 14).

> **Be Organized!**   I hear many complaints about people who hate doing expense reports. This is usually because they wait until the last minute and can never find receipts. I suggest having an envelope with you for each trip just for receipts. If the expense has no receipt (tips, for example), enter it in the Expense application or write a note with date, location, and amount on the envelope when the expense occurs. Then, each evening, make one of your To Do's to enter each receipt in your Palm Expense application.

Payment

To change the type of payment, tap the default type shown. This brings up a list of payment types stored in the system. Select the appropriate type by tapping on it.

Currency

To change the type of currency, tap the default type shown. This brings up a list of currency types stored in the system. Select the appropriate type by tapping on it.

To edit the currency list, follow these steps:

1. Tap Select Currencies. This brings you to the Select Currencies screen (see Figure 10.10).
2. You may select up to five currencies to be displayed in your default list.
3. After you have made all your selections, tap OK.
4. To exit without changes, tap Cancel.

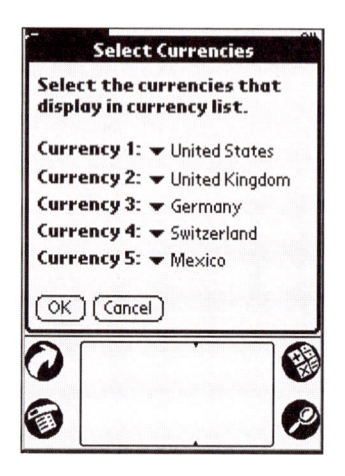

FIGURE 10.10 Select Currencies screen.

Vendor

Enter in the name of the provider of the expense product or service (airline, hotel, restaurant, car rental company, and so on).

> **Set Standards** If you use a common name here, you can search for it more easily. Let's say you want to find all the Delta Airlines listings. Make sure you always enter the name Delta so that you can use the Find utility (see Lesson 14) to locate all the expenses associated with that name.

City

Enter the name of the city where the expense occurred if applicable.

Attendees

If you tap Attendees, you will go the Attendees entry screen (see Figure 10.11). Enter the names of the attendees if applicable.

FIGURE 10.11 Attendees entry screen.

> **Save Time** If the attendees are names already in your Address Book, you can tap Lookup. This brings up a list of all the names in your Address Book. You can then select a name by tapping it and then tapping Add. This adds the name to your Attendee list automatically.

Add a Note to an Entry

If you wish to add a note to your expense entry, tap Note. You can then enter any additional notes you wish. After you have completed the note, tap OK to accept. If you decide you don't want to include the note, tap Delete. You are prompted to confirm before the note is deleted.

Menu Commands

Menu commands are additional capabilities for a given application. To view the menu commands, tap the Menu soft button located at the lower-right section of your display, next to the Graffiti pad. You have several menu commands available for Expense (see Figure 10.12):

Menu Command—Record

Figure 10.12 Menu commands—expense, record.

Delete Item

Deletes the selected expense item. You are prompted to confirm before the item is deleted.

Purge

Deletes an entire category (see Figure 10.13). To use this feature, select the category you want to purge by tapping it. Then tap Purge.

FIGURE 10.13   Purge Categories screen.

> **Warning Will Robinson! Danger!**   You will *not* be prompted to confirm prior to purging a category. This will remove all expenses associated with this category. Use this feature very carefully!

Menu Command—Options

These are system options you can change and other information that applies only to the Expense program (see Figure 10.14). These include setting preferences (see Figure 10.15) and adding a new currency designation.

FIGURE 10.14 Menu commands—Expense, Options.

PREFERENCES

FIGURE 10.15 Preferences screen.

USE AUTOMATIC FILL WHEN ENTERING DATA
Enables you to select to use the Automatic Fill when entering data and to specify a default currency.

APPLICATIONS—EXPENSE   131

> **Fill 'er Up! Use the Automatic Fill Feature!** This feature automatically fills in certain fields such as Vendor and City based on previous entries. It can be a real timesaver.

CUSTOM CURRENCIES

Create your own currency list (see Figure 10.16) with up to four entries by tapping each box and entering the data in the fields provided (see Figure 10.17).

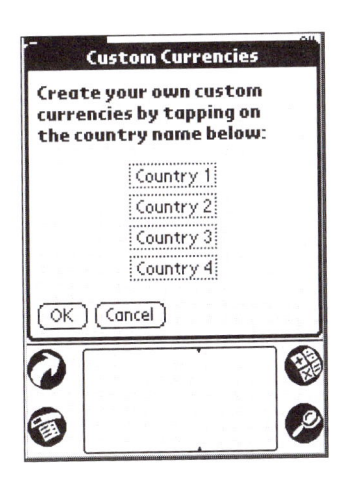

FIGURE 10.16 Custom Currencies screen.

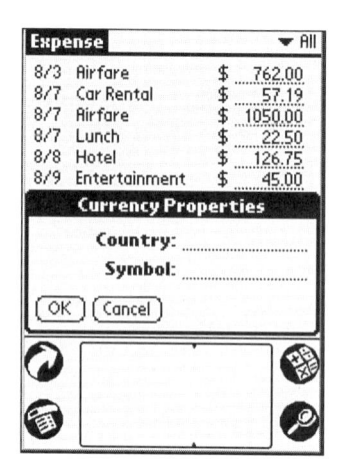

FIGURE 10.17 Currency Properties screen.

ABOUT EXPENSE

This tells you the version number of the Expense program you are using.

In this lesson, you learned how to use your Palm to track expenses. In the next lesson, you learn how to use the Calculator.

Lesson 11

Applications —Calculator

In this lesson, you learn how to use the Calculator program that comes with your Palm.

Using the Calculator

In addition to the many great programs discussed so far, your Palm also includes a full-function calculator (see Figure 11.1). Just one less thing you now have to carry. Let's talk about how to use the basic functions like addition and division, along with the memory functions and some other great features.

Figure 11.1 The Calculator icon.

To start the Calculator program, follow these steps:

1. Turn on the Palm.
2. Tap the Calculator soft button located in the lower-right section of the main display, next to the Graffiti Pad (see Figure 11.2).

LESSON 11

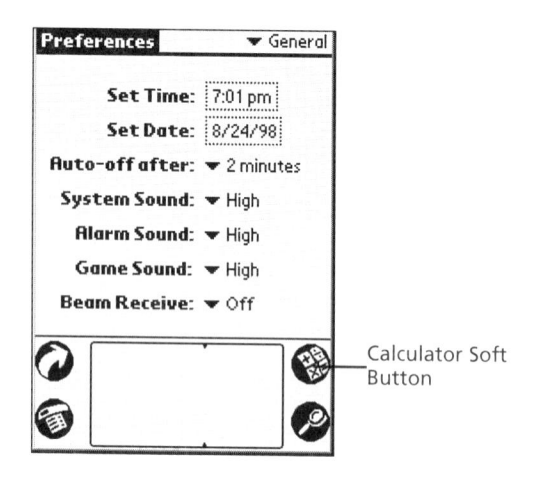

FIGURE 11.2 Calculator soft button.

3. You should now see the main Calculator screen (see Figure 11.3).

Figure 11.3 Calculator screen.

> **Get the Point** You can use your finger or the Stylus to enter data into the calculator. The onscreen buttons were designed to be used like a regular calculator.

> **Quick Start** If you plan to use the calculator a great deal, consider programming one of the hard application buttons (see Lesson 5) on the lower part of your unit with this function. It will save you a step or two in the future.

ADDITION

To perform addition, use the Stylus to tap the appropriate keys. For example:

1. Tap the C button to clear the memory.
2. Tap 250.
3. Tap the + button.
4. Tap 125.
5. Tap the = button.
6. The display should read **375**.

SUBTRACTION

To perform subtraction, use the Stylus to tap the appropriate keys. For example:

1. Tap the C button to clear the memory.
2. Tap 250.
3. Tap the − button.

4. Tap 100.
   5. Tap the = button.
   6. The display should read **150**.

Multiplication

To perform multiplication, use the Stylus to tap the appropriate keys. For example:

   1. Tap the C button to clear the memory.
   2. Tap 250.
   3. Tap the × button.
   4. Tap 10.
   5. Tap the = button.
   6. The display should read **2500**.

Division

To perform division, use the Stylus to tap the appropriate keys. For example:

   1. Tap the C button to clear the memory
   2. Tap 250.
   3. Tap the ÷ button.
   4. Tap 10.
   5. Tap the = button.
   6. The display should read **25**.

ADDITIONAL FUNCTION KEYS

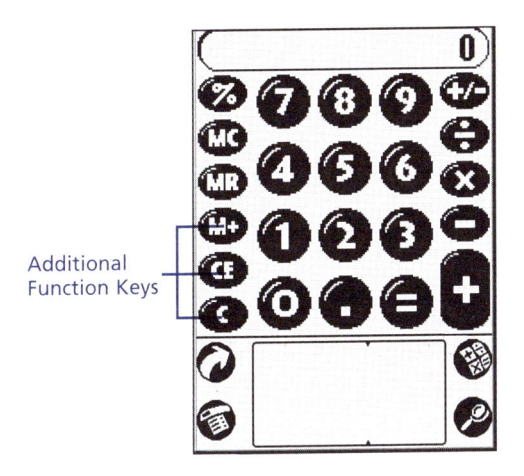

FIGURE 11.4   Additional function keys.

- Clear   The Clear button clears the entire calculation you were performing, enabling you to start from scratch.

- Clear Entry   The Clear Entry button clears only the last number you entered during your calculation. This is so you don't have to start a lengthy calculation from scratch if you make a mistake.

- Memory Store (M+)   The Memory Store button puts the value on the display into memory for later use. You can bring the value back using Memory Recall.

> **No Effect**   The act of storing a value has no effect on any calculations you perform.

- Memory Recall (MR)   The Memory Recall button restores the value you last placed in memory.

- Memory Clear (MC)   The Memory Clear button clears the value from the stored memory.

- Percentage   Just as it sounds, the % button is used to calculate as percentages.

- Positive and Negative numbers (+/–)   The (+/–) button changes the current value displayed from positive to negative or from negative to positive.

To enter a negative number, first enter the number, then (+/–). To change the number back to positive, tap (+/–) again.

Menu Commands

FIGURE 11.5   The Menu icon.

Menu commands are additional capabilities for a given application. To view the menu commands, tap the Menu soft button located on the lower-right section of your display, next to the Graffiti Pad. You have the following several menu commands available for the Calculator.

Menu Commands—Edit
Lesson 14 describes these commands.

Menu Commands—Options
These are system options you change or other information that will apply only to the Calculator program (see Figure 11.6). These include the font and the way information is displayed.

APPLICATIONS—CALCULATOR 139

FIGURE 11.6   Menu commands—options.

RECENT CALCULATIONS

Here's a great feature. Unlike many other calculators, this program keeps track of your activity and displays the most recent calculations upon request (see Figure 11.7). It is similar to having paper tape.

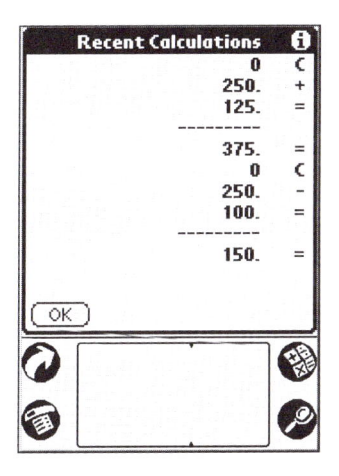

FIGURE 11.7   Recent Calculations display.

> **Plus and Minus** Although this is a handy feature, keep in mind that it displays only the most recent series of calculations that can be shown on a single screen. It also does not allow copying or pasting. Oh well, nothing's perfect.

About Calculator

This tells you the version number of the Calculator program you are using.

In this lesson, you learned how to use the calculator. In the next lesson, we discuss how to use your Palm to read email.

Lesson 12

Applications —Mail

In this lesson, you learn how use the Mail program to read your email and prepare messages.

Using the Mail Application

Suppose you are traveling and would like to review your mail, but would prefer not to take out and start up your laptop. Or maybe you want quick access to your recent mail while in a meeting.

With Mail you can view electronic mail from your Palm. You can also create and send new message easily. The system is designed to replicate the email that resides on your PC. Let's step through each process.

> **Not Your PC's Email** Viewing email on your Palm is not the same as viewing from the desktop. Message size is limited and attachments can't be viewed.

I should note here that I am only discussing use of the Palm Mail program (see Figure 12.1) in this lesson. To receive new mail for viewing, you need to set up your PC desktop email program to synchronize with the Palm during the HotSync process or to connect the Palm to a modem (such as the optional Palm modem available from 3Com or your Palm reseller), which you use to dial directly to your email provider.

LESSON 12

FIGURE 12.1 The Mail icon.

STARTING MAIL

To start the Mail program, follow these steps:

1. Turn on the Palm.
2. Tap the Applications soft button.
3. Tap Mail.
4. The main Mail screen appears (see Figure 12.2).

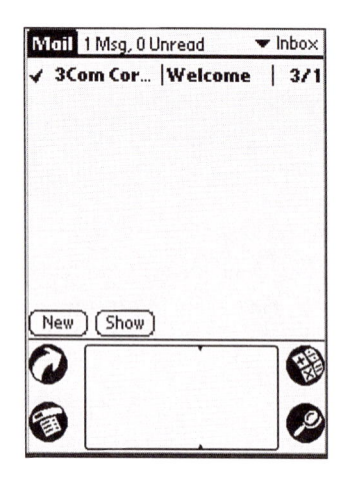

FIGURE 12.2 Main Mail screen.

VIEWING AN EXISTING ENTRY

To view the contents of an existing message, follow these steps:

1. Tap message. At this point, you may either indicate you are done reading the message, create a reply, or delete the message.

APPLICATIONS—MAIL   143

> **Long Messages**   If the message is longer than one screen, you can move up and down the page either using the Page Up/Down buttons located at the bottom of the Palm between the hard application buttons, or using the soft slide control located on the right side of the main display. Position your Stylus on the slide control and move up and down.

2. If you have completed reading the message and wish to save it, tap Done. This returns you to the main Mail screen.

3. If you would like to answer this message, tap Reply. This takes you to the Reply Options menu screen (see Figure 12.3). At this point, you decide to whom you want to reply and whether the original text should be included.

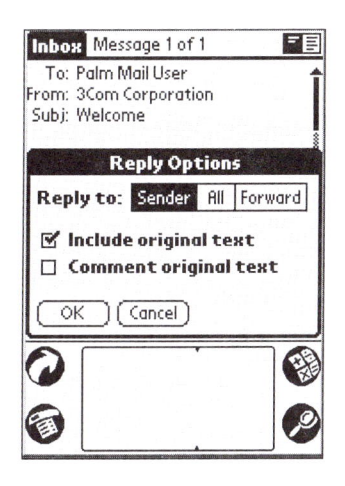

FIGURE 12.3   Reply Options screen.

4. Decide whether you want to reply just to the sender, to all copied on the message, or whether you want to forward the email to someone else.

144   LESSON 12

> **Reply to All?**   Think carefully before choosing Reply to All. I have heard many stories of people would wrote a reply in haste, accidentally including material not meant for everyone. Choosing Sender tends to be the safer choice.

5. If you wish to remove the message from the system, tap Delete. You are prompted to confirm before the message is deleted.

ADDING A NEW EMAIL MESSAGE

To create a new email message, follow these steps:

1. Tap New. The New Message screen appears (see Figure 12.4). You now fill in to **To:**, **CC:**, **Subj:** (Subject), and **Body:** sections of the message where applicable.

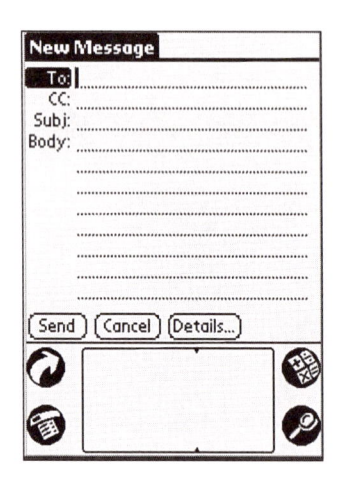

FIGURE 12.4   New Message screen.

> **More Space** If you plan to enter an expanded amount of information for any of these fields, tap the field name itself. The screen automatically expands, giving you plenty of room to work. You can also use the LookUp utility to find the name of someone in your Address Book.

2. Type your message.

3. After you have completed your message and are satisfied with the contents, tap Send. This automatically places the message in the Outbox. The message will be sent the next time you HotSync.

4. If you decide to exit the message without saving, tap Cancel.

5. If you would like to see the details associated with this new message, tap Details. This takes you to the Message Details screen (see Figure 12.5). From this screen, your choices include changing the priority and adding a Signature to the message.

FIGURE 12.5   Message Details screen.

Lesson 12

> **Email Signature** Signature refers to a file you create that contains information about you to be placed at the bottom of the message. Most people include their name and email address; others include their full company name address, telephone number, and so on. It is both a timesaver and good way to ensure that any important information about you is sent with the message. See the "Menu Commands—Options" section in this lesson for instructions on how to create the signature text.

6. Select the priority level (Normal, High, Low) at which you want the message sent.

7. Select any BCC or "Blind Carbon Copy" recipients. You can specify that the message be sent to additional people, without indicating this in the main part of the message. If you enable BCC, the program returns to the Message Creation screen with the BCC added. Enter the additional addresses at this time.

> Using BCC is good for sending messages to lists of people. The message arrives, but the receiver does not know who else received the message and can respond only to the sender. This helps to keep other persons' email addresses private.

8. Use Signature to add your signature file to the message.

9. Choose Confirm Read if you want a confirmation that the receiver has read your message.

10. Choose Confirm Delivery if you want confirmation that your message has been delivered.

11. After you have complete your reply, forward, or new message, tap Send. This places the message in the Mail program's Outbox.

Menu Commands

Menu commands are additional capabilities for a given application. To view the menu commands, tap the Menu soft button located on the lower-right section of your display, next to the Graffiti Pad. You have several menu commands available for the Mail program.

Menu Commands—Message

Two Graffiti shortcuts enable you to move or to perform a command with two strokes (see Figure 12.6) They are as follows:

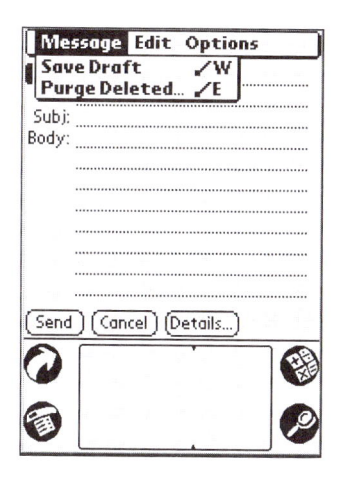

Figure 12.6 Menu commands—Message.

- New   Using this command automatically brings you to the New Message screen.

- Purge Deleted   This command automatically purges all messages you have marked to delete.

Menu Commands—Edit

Lesson 14 describes these commands.

Lesson 12

Menu Commands—Options

These are system options you can change and other information that applies only to the Mail program (see Figure 12.7). These include the font and how information displays.

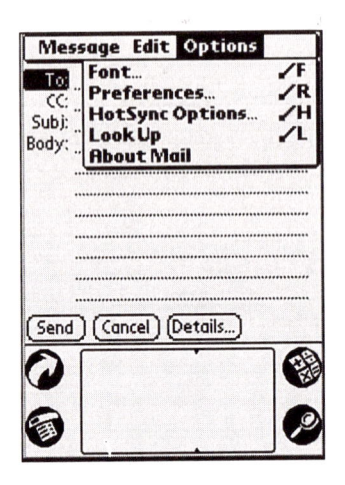

FIGURE 12.7   Menu commands—Options.

Font

Select the font you wish from the list provided.

Preferences

From the main menu, you can also set preferences for this application alone (see Figure 12.8).

APPLICATIONS—MAIL   149

FIGURE 12.8   Preferences screen.

- Confirm deleted messages   Keep the box checked if you want the system to confirm before messages are deleted.

- Signature text   This is where you enter your signature text. If you instruct the application to use your signature file, this text appears at the bottom of the message.

HOTSYNC OPTIONS

This is where you decide which message will be sent and received during the HotSync process (see Figure 12.9).

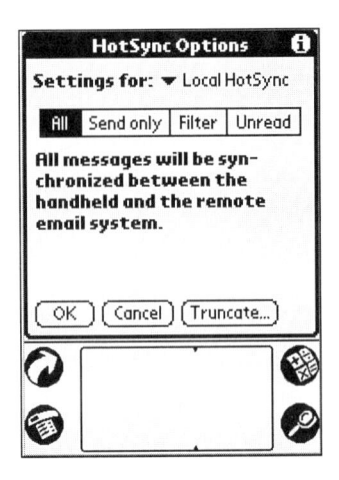

FIGURE 12.9   HotSync Options screen.

- **All**   This syncs all messages between the Palm and your remote or desktop email program.

- **Send only**   This syncs only the messages in your Outbox to the remote or desktop email program. No messages will be received.

- **Filter**   You can set specific parameters to receive mail. These include whether all high-priority messages should be received and whether messages should be sent or received based on the **To:**, **From:**, or **Subj:** line.

> **Filters**   The email program is designed to read the text of a message as it is being received. Filters are programs that execute commands based on parameters you choose. You can elect to ignore all messages coming from a certain email address, for example.

- **Unread**   This tells the system to bring over only copies of unread messages from the remote email program.

- **Truncate messages**   The Mail program will truncate all messages after a certain amount of characters. To select the size, tap

APPLICATIONS—MAIL   151

Truncate. You will see the Truncate Options screen (see Figure 12.10). Select the level of truncation (between 250–8000 characters) from the list provided.

FIGURE 12.10   Truncate Options screen.

> **Truncate**   To cut off the amount of characters received upon reaching a certain level. This is normally done to save storage space on the Palm.

> **Size Does Matter**   Remember that the larger the truncate size you choose, the fewer messages you can store on your Palm. You need to study the quantity and size of your messages and then decide what truncate level is best. If you get a lot of small messages or many large messages, you may want to consider adding more memory to your unit.

LookUp

This enables you to search for a specific message.

About Mail

This tells you the version number of the Mail program you are using.

Using the Draft and Filed Folders

You have additional folders in which you can store messages. Using these folders can help you sort messages and find them quicker. Let's discuss how to use each one.

Placing Messages in the Draft Folder

During the creation of a message, you can elect to save a message to the Draft folder instead of placing it in the Outbox. You can review this message at a later time, at which point you can edit, delete, or send it.

To place a message in the Draft folder, follow these steps:

1. During the creation of a new message, tap Cancel.
2. The Save Draft dialog box appears (see Figure 12.11). To save the message to the Draft folder, tap Yes.

FIGURE 12.11 Save Draft dialog box.

APPLICATIONS—MAIL 153

PLACING MESSAGES IN THE FILED FOLDER

You can place a message you are reading into the Filed folder. You may wish to do this to remove it from your Unread message list.

To place a message in the Filed folder, follow these steps:

1. While reading the message, tap the Menu soft button. The drop-down menus appears (see Figure 12.12).

FIGURE 12.12   Menu command—Message drop-down menu.

2. From the Message menu, select File. The message will then be placed in the Filed folder.

> **No Place to Go**   After you place a message in the Filed folder, it can never again be moved. It can only be deleted. When you execute the File command, you are given the option to keep a copy in your Inbox. Although this means that you would have two copies on the Palm (taking up additional memory), you may want to exercise this option on certain occasions.

> **Process Messages Quickly** To avoid overloading the Palm memory, I recommend reviewing your messages often. Read, reply, or delete as needed. Then HotSync to empty your Outbox.

In this lesson, you learned how to read and reply to your mail and send new messages. The next lesson covers the security features available on your Palm.

Lesson 13

Applications —Security

In this lesson, you learn about setting the security features on your Palm, such as hiding private records and assigning passwords.

Using the Security Features

Security. It's a fact of life—and data. You may have personal or sensitive information on your Palm you don't want anyone else to see. Therefore, you may wish to use the security provided with the Palm.

Think about it. You give your Palm to someone to show him how it works without even a second thought. What if there is something in there you don't want him to know about, like a credit card number or a personal memo? Or what if your Palm is lost or stolen? Be sure to protect your data.

The security program gives you the option of several levels of security. You can hide certain files without password control or you can require password entry before they can be viewed. You can even lock the entire contents of the Palm. This means if your Palm is lost or stolen, your most valuable information is still protected. The level you choose is up to you.

> **It's 8 o'clock. Do you know where your Palm is?**
> Remember, you have a lot invested in your Palm. The best security is to carry your Palm at all times and never let it out of your sight. Be careful not to place it on a desk or counter and then walk away.

To start the Security application, follow these steps:

1. Turn on the Palm.
2. Tap the Applications soft menu button.
3. Tap the Security program icon (see Figure 13.1).
4. The Security main screen appears (see Figure 13.2).

FIGURE 13.1 The Security icon.

FIGURE 13.2 Main Security screen.

From here, things you can decide whether to show or hide your private records and set up your password.

Private Records

In previous lessons, we have discussed marking records private. When you create a record, you have the ability to designate it Private. Private records can be viewed only after you enter a password (see the section titled "Assigning a Password").

These records can still be viewed, however, unless you tell the Palm that you want your private records hidden from view. If you select Hide for these records, they will be hidden from everyone until you go back to the Security program and instruct it to Show (unhide) them.

This may seem a little complicated. Let me try to explain. You have the following two levels of security here:

1. You could mark a record as Private and *not* assign a password but instruct the system to hide all private records. This means that if you hand your Palm to someone, he won't see your private records *unless* he goes to the Security program and changes the Hide/Show setting to Show.

2. You could mark a record Private, assign a password, and instruct the system to hide all private records. This would then require you to enter the password after instructing the system to Show private records. This is the highest level of security.

ASSIGNING A PASSWORD

Use this screen to assign and enter a password. Tap the Unassigned button to bring up the Password Entry screen (see Figure 13.3). You will be asked to enter the password a second time to confirm it.

FIGURE 13.3 Password entry screen.

Changing an Existing Password

After you have assigned a password, you can change it at any time. Tap Assigned on the Security screen. You will see the Password Security screen (see Figure 13.4). Enter the existing password. You can then change your password, leave it as is, or delete it completely.

FIGURE 13.4 Password Security screen.

FORGOTTEN PASSWORD

If you forget your password, you can use this feature to delete the password from memory.

> **Let's Play Password** If you decide to delete your password, be warned! As a precaution, the system will delete *all* records marked Private at the same time!

TURN OFF AND LOCK DEVICE

This command turns off the power to the Palm and lock the device if you have previously set a password. You will be prompted to confirm before the system shuts off. To get back into the system, you must then enter your password.

> **Don't Forget!** After you set a password and lock your system, you must enter a password to get back in. If you forget your password at this stage, your only option is a hard reset, which will wipe out all records in the system. This means you will lose any data entered into the Palm that you have not backed up. A HotSync will restore your existing data.

MENU COMMANDS—OPTIONS

These are system options you can change and other information that will applies to the Security program (see Figure 13.5).

FIGURE 13.5 Menu commands—Security options.

ABOUT SECURITY

This tells you the version number of the Security program you are using.

In this lesson, you learned about setting and using the security features available in the Palm. The next lesson reviews some additional Palm software features not discussed so far.

Lesson 14

Additional Palm Programs and Utilities

In this lesson, you learn to use some additional programs, including the Find utility and the Edit section of the Menu commands.

More Palm Programs

The folks at Palm have included a few other elements that we have not discussed so far. These include a search program and a program for calculating the amount of available memory in your system. Let's go through each one, step by step.

Find

Find is a great little search program. It searches the entire contents of the Palm looking for the word your specify.

To start Find, follow these steps:

1. Turn on the Palm.
2. Tap the Find soft button, located at the lower-right portion of the display, next to the Graffiti Pad (see Figure 14.1).

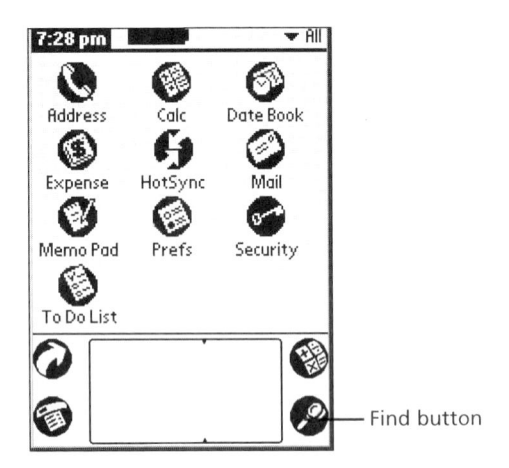

FIGURE 14.1 Find soft button.

3. You will now see the Find main screen (see Figure 14.2). Enter the word to search for.

FIGURE 14.2 Main Find screen.

4. The system will search each application that accepts data and return a summary of where the word was found, if at all. You can tap the summary to see the record that contains the word.

> **Seek and You Shall Find** Find is a great utility for locating a variety of things. If you can't remember the date of your last haircut, for example, enter haircut in the Find program, and it will list all occurrences of your haircuts listed anywhere in your Palm.

MENU COMMANDS—EDIT

The Edit commands under the Menu utility are common across most of the applications they are available for (see Figure 14.3). There are the five commands typical of a word processor or other common application.

FIGURE 14.3 Menu commands—Edit.

- Undo Moves back one step.

- Cut Deletes the highlighted data from the screen, but save it in memory.

- Copy Copies the highlighted data into memory.

- Paste Places the data stored in memory at the point where the cursor is located.

- Select All   Highlights all the data onscreen. In addition, you can access the soft keyboard and Graffiti Help screen from here.
- Keyboard   This brings up the soft keyboard (see Figure 14.4).

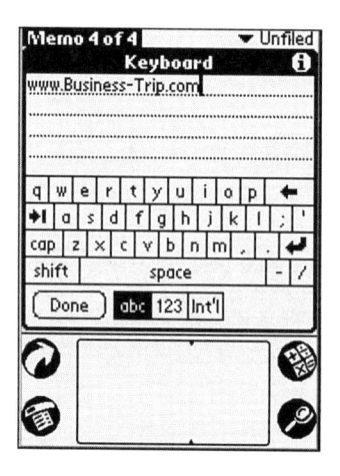

FIGURE 14.4   Soft keyboard.

- Graffiti Help   This brings up the Graffiti character Help screen (see Figure 14.5).

FIGURE 14.5   Graffiti character Help screen.

Checking the Memory Status of Your Palm

The Memory program in Palm Version 2.0 is a utility that looks at all the programs and data and presents an onscreen summary of how much memory you have available. This can help you decide whether a memory upgrade may be in order. It also enables you to delete applications from the system.

To start the Memory program and check your available memory, follow these steps:

1. Turn on the Palm.
2. Tap the Applications soft button located at the lower-left portion of the display next to the Graffiti Pad.
3. Tap the Memory program icon.
4. The system will automatically do a system analysis and present the summary on screen.

In the Memory program, you can delete applications and decide how you want applications displayed.

Delete Applications

To delete an application, tap Delete apps. You will see a screen containing a list of applications that can be deleted. Tap an application name to delete. You are asked to confirm before the deletion occurs.

List Display

You can also select how you want the list of applications to display in the summary. You can choose alphabetical by application name, or by size of file.

Checking the Memory Status of Your Palm

If you have a Palm III or if you have upgraded from Palm OS 2.0 to 3.0, you will notice the Memory program in the Palm OS version 3.0 is similar to the 2.0 version. However, access is through a Menu command rather than an icon.

To start the Memory program in version 3.0, follow these steps:

1. Turn on the Palm.

2. Tap the Applications soft button located at the lower-left portion of the display next to the Graffiti Pad.

3. Tap the Menu soft button located below the soft applications button on the lower-left portion of the display, next to the Graffiti Pad.

4. From the Menu commands, App list, tap Info. You will see a memory status display (see Figure 14.6).

FIGURE 14.6   Memory status display.

You will also notice the option to delete applications is no longer part of the Memory program.

Deleting Apps

The Delete Apps program in the Palm OS version 3.0 is similar to the 2.0 version except that access is again through a Menu command rather than an icon.

ADDITIONAL PALM PROGRAMS AND UTILITIES 167

To start the Delete Apps program in version 3.0, follow these steps:

1. Turn on the Palm.

2. Tap the Applications soft button located at the lower-left portion of the display next to the Graffiti Pad.

3. Tap the Menu soft button located below the soft applications button on the lower-left portion of the display next to the Graffiti Pad.

4. From the Menu commands, App list, tap Delete.

MENU COMMANDS—MAIN APPLICATIONS SCREEN

As you can see from the previous sections, one of the changes that occurred in the Palm OS version 3.0 is the addition of new Menu commands available from the main Applications screen (see Figure 14.7). We have already covered the Delete Apps and Info commands from the App section. Let's discuss the rest.

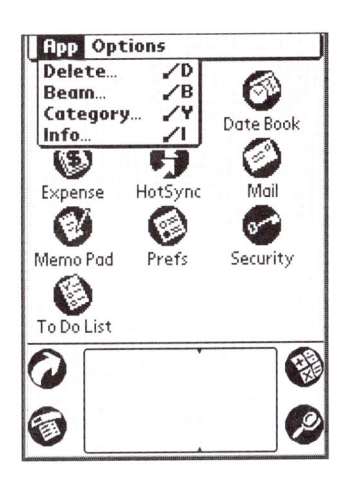

FIGURE 14.7 Menu commands—Main Applications screen—App.

Menu Commands—Main Applications Screen—App

- **Delete** Delete was previously discussed in this lesson.

- **Beam** You can beam an application to another Palm. Select that application and tap Beam. Copy-protected applications cannot be beamed.

- **Category** Use Category to assign each application to its own category. To change a category, tap the default category next to the application you wish to change. Then tap the new category from the list provided.

- **Info** Info was previously discussed in this lesson.

Menu Commands—Main Applications Screen—Options

These are option commands that apply only to the main Applications screen in the Palm OS 3.0 (see Figure 14.8).

FIGURE 14.8 Menu Commands—Main Applications screen—Options.

PREFERENCES

Under Preferences, you can opt to have the system remember the last category. If you uncheck this, the default category ALL will always appear.

You can also change the main Applications screen display to show a list with small icons rather than large ones (see Figure 14.9).

FIGURE 14.9 Alternate main Applications screen.

ABOUT APPLICATIONS

This tells you the version number of the program. Tap OK to exit.

GIRAFFE GAME

The Giraffe is a simple game that comes with your Palm to help you learn Graffiti. It requires you to enter Graffiti strokes to play.

You should use this game to practice your Graffiti entry skills.

To start the Giraffe game, follow these steps:

1. Turn on your Palm.

2. Tap the Applications soft button located at the lower-right portion of the display next to the Graffiti Pad.

3. Tap the Giraffe game icon.
4. Follow the instructions.

In this lesson, you learned about the additional programs and utilities available in your Palm. In the next lesson, you will connect your HotSync cradle and install the Desktop software.

LESSON 15

INITIAL PC HARDWARE AND SOFTWARE SETUP

In this lesson, you connect the HotSync cradle to your PC and install the Desktop software.

SETTING UP YOUR HARDWARE

We have spent all the previous lessons working on the actual Palm unit, operating system, and programs. Eventually, you will want to use HotSync to transfer data to your PC for updates and backup and for use with other applications.

Backing up is very important. Should your Palm data be lost, a quick HotSync will have it back to normal in no time. You can also use your PC to easily enter large amounts of data from other applications. Before you HotSync, you first must connect the cradle to your PC and install the Desktop software. Let's take these one step at a time.

PC REQUIREMENTS

Palm Computing recommends that you verify that your PC meets the following requirements before you connect the HotSync cable:

Hardware	IBM-compatible 386 PC or higher
Operating system	Windows 95, Windows NT, Windows 98, Windows 3.1x, or Windows for Workgroups
RAM (minimum)	8MB (16MB recommended)

Hard disk	10MB for Windows 95/NT 4.0/98. 13MB for Windows 3.1x
Serial port	One (as explained later in this chapter)
CD-ROM	Present, if using CD to install
Mouse	Present

HotSync Cradle

The HotSync cradle that comes with your Palm is a small, plastic device with a serial cable attached, and is designed to hold the Palm at a 45-degree angle (see Figure 15.1). The HotSync button is located on the front on the lower-right side.

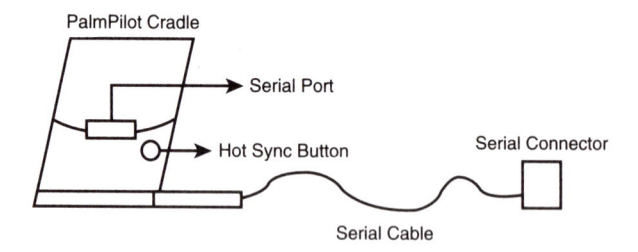

FIGURE 15.1 Palm Pilot Cradle.

Connecting the HotSync Cradle

Connecting the cradle is very easy. Just follow these steps:

1. Turn off the PC.

> **Power Off** It is highly recommended that you not attach cables or do any other work on a PC unless the power is turned off.

2. Attach the serial connector at the end of the cable to the open serial port on the PC (see Figure 15.2). If the serial port is a 25-pin connector, connect the 25-pin to 9-pin adapter provided by 3Com to the 9-pin connector on the end of the cable first. Make sure the connector is secured firmly in place.

3. You can then turn the PC power back on.

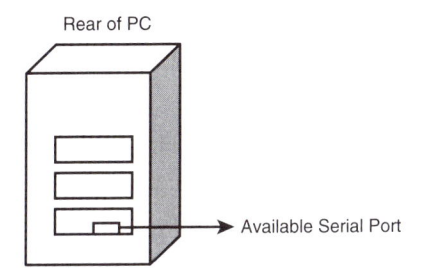

FIGURE 15.2 Rear of PC.

> **Serial Port** A communication board located inside the PC that allows outside devices to connect or "talk" to the PC. Other devices that connect to a PC through the serial port include a mouse and a modem.

You are not quite ready to HotSync yet. You must first install the Desktop software.

INSTALLING THE DESKTOP SOFTWARE

The Desktop software contains several different elements. These include the HotSync Manager, Expense Report program, and Palm Install Tool. You will want to install all or most of this software on your PC.

The software should be on a CD-ROM that came with your Palm. Insert that CD into your CD-ROM drive. The install procedure should start automatically. If it does not, use the Windows Start, Run command to locate and execute the Setup.exe (for the Palm 2.0 Desktop CD), the Autorun.exe (for the Palm 3.0 Desktop file that you can download from the Palm Web site), or a similar file. The opening screen for the Palm Desktop Installer program should appear (see Figure 15.3).

> **No CD-ROM?** If your PC does not have CD-ROM, you will need to contact 3Com/Palm to order the 3.5-inch disk version of the Palm Desktop software. See the Palm Web site for more information.

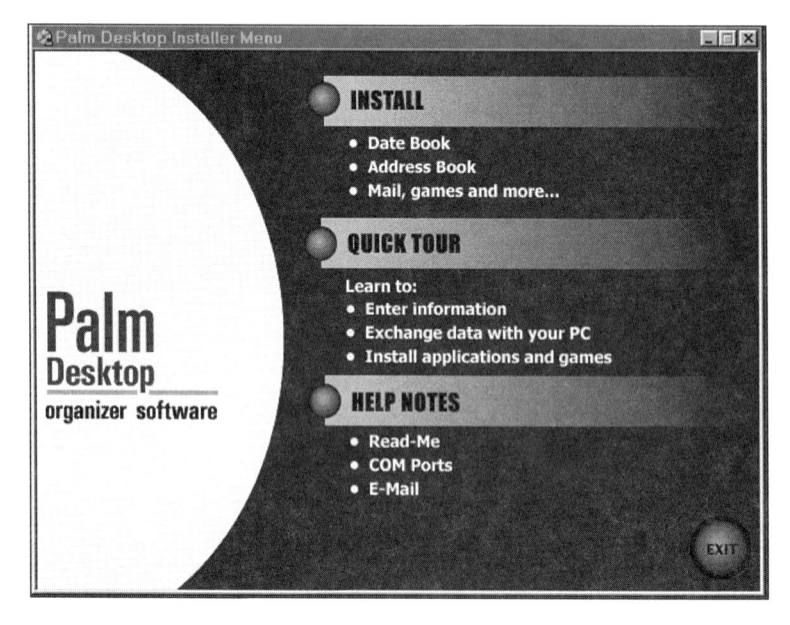

FIGURE 15.3 Palm Desktop 3.0 Installer screen.

INITIAL **PC** HARDWARE AND SOFTWARE SETUP   175

> **Latest Version**   You should verify that you have the latest version of the Desktop software. Go to the Palm Computing Web site (http://www.palm.com) and search for the downloads page or other section that provides information on the latest available software versions. You might even be able to download the latest version for free (see the Web site). If you do download a new version, follow the instructions provided on how to start the Installer program.

You now have several options: install the software, take a tour, or view some additional notes.

> **Don't Put the Palm in the Cradle Yet!**   Palm Computing recommends that the Palm unit *not* be in the cradle during the beginning of the Desktop install. Watch the screen and follow the instructions.

- **Install**

    Click Install to install the Palm Desktop software. Follow the instructions to tell the system what software you want to load. If you are a first-time user, you may want to install all the available files. You can always remove the ones you don't need at a later time. If you are installing over an older version of the Desktop software, the system should handle this and your existing data will not be affected.

> **Error Message** You may receive an error message, depending on what version of Microsoft Word and Excel you are running and how you installed them. Don't worry. The Installer program is set up to look for specific destination files for Word and Excel. If it does not find them, it will place the files in an alternative location. Read the Readme.txt file that comes with the Installer program for more details.

- **Quick Tour**

    The Quick Tour is a multimedia show that takes you through some of the Palm basics.

- **Helpful Notes**

    This brings up a new window with icons for several .txt files. These might be worth a read.

After successfully completing the install, you will be ready to use the Desktop and HotSync software.

> **Don't Perform a HotSync Yet!** Please wait until we have stepped through the basic Desktop applications before performing a HotSync. Lesson 20 covers the HotSync process.

In this lesson, you learned how to connect the Palm cradle and install the PC software. The next lesson covers the Desktop Address Book application.

LESSON 16
DESKTOP SOFTWARE— ADDRESS BOOK

In this lesson, you learn to use the Desktop Address Book to add new addresses and to look up existing ones.

You will find the Desktop Address Book very similar to the Address Book on the Palm. This should make entering data on the desktop very easy.

OPENING THE ADDRESS BOOK

To get to the Desktop Address Book, follow these steps:

1. Start the Palm Desktop application from the Windows Start/Run, Start/Programs or by using the Palm Desktop icon on your Windows desktop. This brings up the main palm Desktop screen (see Figure 16.1).

2. Click the Address Book button located on the left side of the screen. This brings up the main Palm Address Book screen (see Figure 16.2).

Lesson 16

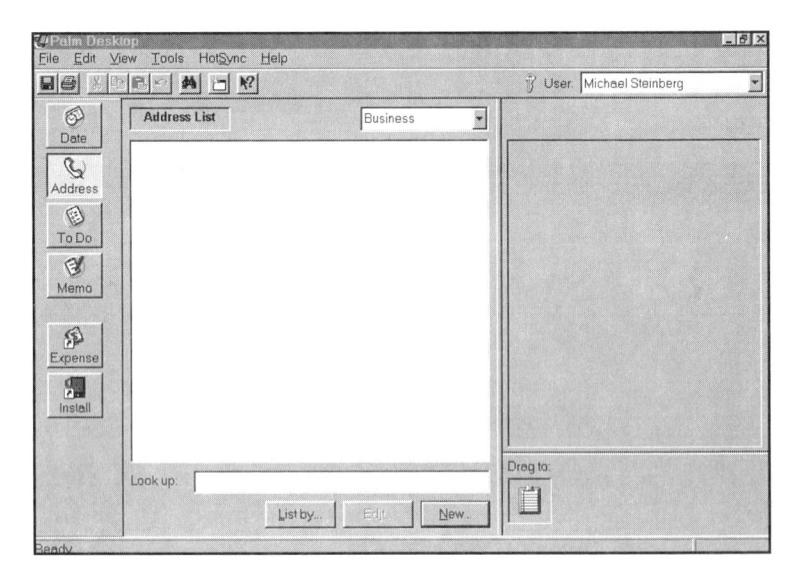

Figure 16.1 Main Desktop screen.

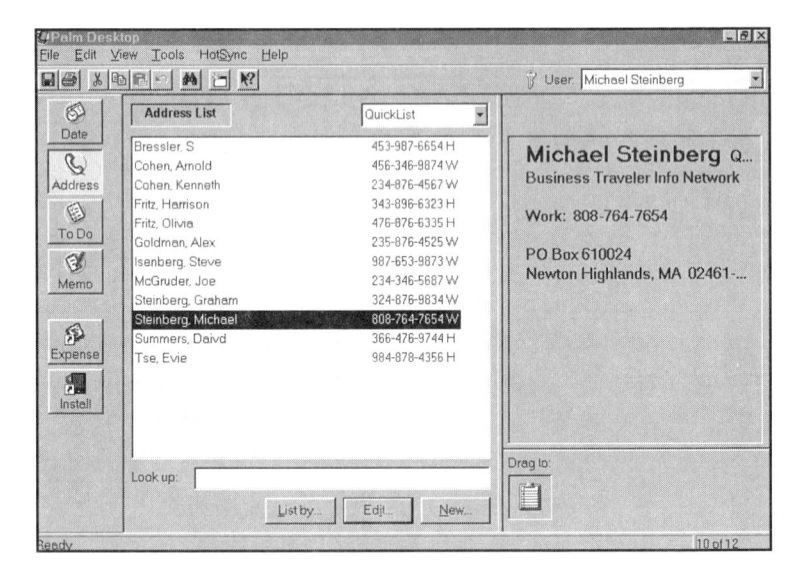

Figure 16.2 Main Desktop Address Book screen.

Adding a New Entry

Adding new names to your Address Book is easy. There are three ways to begin a new entry. To begin entering a new name, you can

- Move the mouse to the Edit pull-down menu and select New Address, or

- From the keyboard, press Cntrl-N, or

- Click the New button located at the lower-middle portion of the screen, or

- Click the New Item icon on the button bar at the top of the display.

Any of these takes you to the main Edit Address data entry screen (see Figure 16.3). The screen has three tabs: Name, Address, and Note. I suggest that you make at least one sample entry at this time.

Navigating the Name Screen

Start with the Name screen. Enter the appropriate information for each line shown:

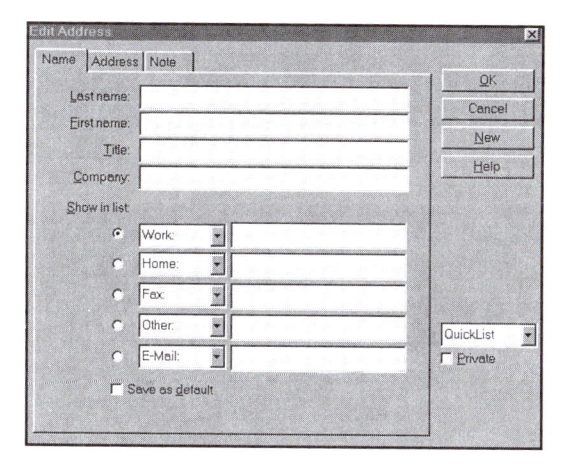

FIGURE 16.3   Edit Address data entry screen.

- Last Name
- First Name
- Title
- Company
- Telephone–Work
- Telephone–Home
- Fax
- Pager
- E-Mail
- Mobile
- Main
- Other

For the telephone-related categories, you can choose each field from a list. To see the list, tap the default that has a down-arrow next to it. The list of available categories appears. To choose a different category, tap that category.

Navigating the Address Screen

Next, move to the Address screen (see Figure 16.4) by clicking on the Address tab at the top of the display. Enter the appropriate information for each line shown:

- Address
- City
- State
- Country
- Custom 1
- Custom 2
- Custom 3
- Custom 4

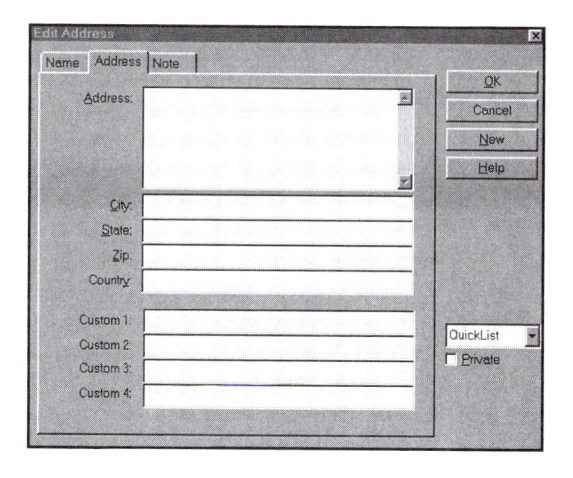

FIGURE 16.4   Address screen.

USING THE NOTE SCREEN

Finally, move to the Note screen by clicking the Note tab at the top of the display (see Figure 16.5). Enter a note if applicable.

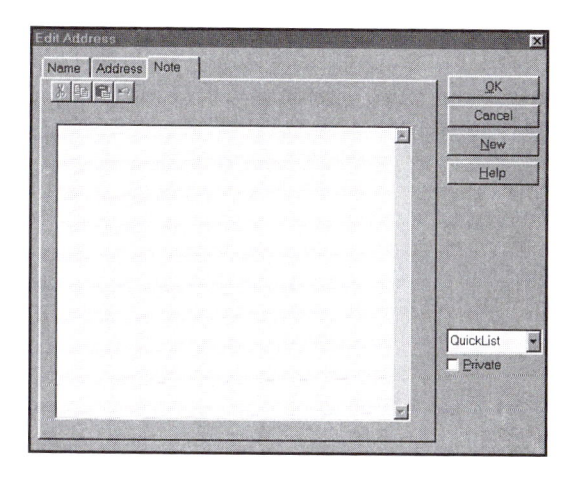

FIGURE 16.5   Note screen.

If you wish to mark the record private, check the Private box. If you wish to assign this record to a specific category, use the mouse to click the down arrow marked QuickList. This will show the entire list of categories available. Choose a new category by clicking on that name. If you want to add a new category, click Edit Categories.

After you have completed entering all the data, click the OK button located at the upper-right portion of the Edit Address dialog box. If you decide to exit without saving the data entered, click the Cancel button. To enter another name, click the New button. If you need assistance, click Help.

> **Collect Business Cards? Use a Scanner!** If you plan to enter large amounts of address information from business cards, consider the purchase of a business card scanner. Several vendors offer scanners with software that allows the scanned data to be automatically entered directly in the Palm Desktop software, which can then be HotSynced to your Palm.

Viewing an Existing Entry

Viewing an existing entry is easy. Follow the steps outlined previously to get back to the main Address Book screen.

You should now see an abbreviated list of entries, arranged alphabetically by last name and including a phone number. This list should include the sample entry you just made.

To view the entire entry, just click on that entry. All the information you entered previously should now be displayed to the right of the abbreviated list of entries. If the information takes up more than one screen, use the up/down arrows or the page slide located at the far right to move as needed.

Find an Existing Entry

You may find that after you have entered many names in the Address Book that it takes too long to scroll up and down to find a particular one. No problem. Address Book has a Look Up feature.

Start at the Main Address Book Screen. At the bottom of the screen below the abbreviated name list, you see the words **Look up** and a field to enter data.

Just begin to enter the last name of the person you are looking for. The program will automatically move to the entry that most closely matches what you type (as you type).

CATEGORIES

As your Address Book gets larger, another way to ease your search is to use Categories. The Categories option enables you to create segments that can be displayed upon request.

Assume, for example, that you have several hundred entries in your Address Book. If you think about it, most of these people will fit into one primary category—for example personal or business. Using categories can make it easier to view your Address Book and locate specific entries.

ASSIGN A CATEGORY

To assign a category to a specific entry, you select it from a default list. Follow these steps:

1. Follow the previously outlined steps to get back to the Main Address Book screen.

2. You should now see an abbreviated list of entries, arranged by last name and including a phone number. This list should include the sample entry you just made.

3. To view the entire entry, just click on that entry. All the information you entered previously should now be displayed in a box on the right side of the screen.

4. In the upper-middle section of the screen, you will see a down arrow with a word (for example: **All**) next to it. Click that arrow.

5. The list of available categories appears.

6. To change the category for this entry, click the new category.

EDIT OR ADD CATEGORIES

If you wish to add, rename, or delete a category, click Edit Categories. You will see the Edit Address Categories screen (see Figure 16.6).

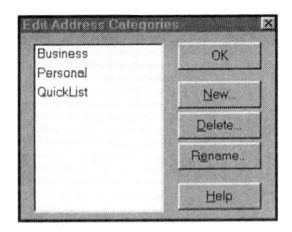

FIGURE 16.6 Edit Address Categories screen.

In the Edit Address Categories screen, you have several options:

ADDING A NEW CATEGORY

To add a new category, follow these steps:

1. Click New.
2. Enter the new category name and click OK.
3. To exit without changes, click Cancel.

RENAMING A CATEGORY

To rename an existing category, follow these steps:

1. Select that category by clicking on it.
2. Click Rename.
3. Enter the new category name and click OK.
4. To exit without changes, click Cancel.

Deleting a Category

To delete an existing category, follow these steps:

1. Select that category by clicking on it.

2. Click Delete.

3. You are asked to confirm before the category is deleted.

> **Think Carefully** If you delete a category in use, the system will ask whether you want to recategorize any associated items to "Unfiled" or delete all the associated items completely. Choose wisely.

In this lesson, you learned how to use the Desktop Address Book. In the next lesson, you learn how to use the Desktop Date Book.

LESSON 17

DESKTOP APPLICATIONS—DATE BOOK

In this lesson, you learn how to add meetings and other events into the Desktop Date Book.

WHAT IS THE DESKTOP DATE BOOK?

Like its Palm companion, the Desktop Date Book is designed to track your daily activities, both personal and business. It keeps a list of your meetings and other events, along with personal information such as birthday reminders.

Because many people purchase a Palm to replace their Filofax or other day planners, the Date Book is a very popular Palm application. The Desktop Date Book program enables you to enter new event information easily, as well as view existing event and general calendar information quickly. It can also be helpful when traveling to meetings or conferences. As you input new contacts, you can automatically transfer them to your desktop system using HotSync. It is a great tool.

OPENING DATE BOOK

To open the Date Book, follow these steps:

1. Start the Palm Desktop application from the Windows Start/Run, Start/Programs or by using the Palm Desktop icon (see Figure 17.1) on your Windows desktop. This brings up the main Palm Desktop screen (see Figure 17.2).

FIGURE 17.1 The Date Book icon.

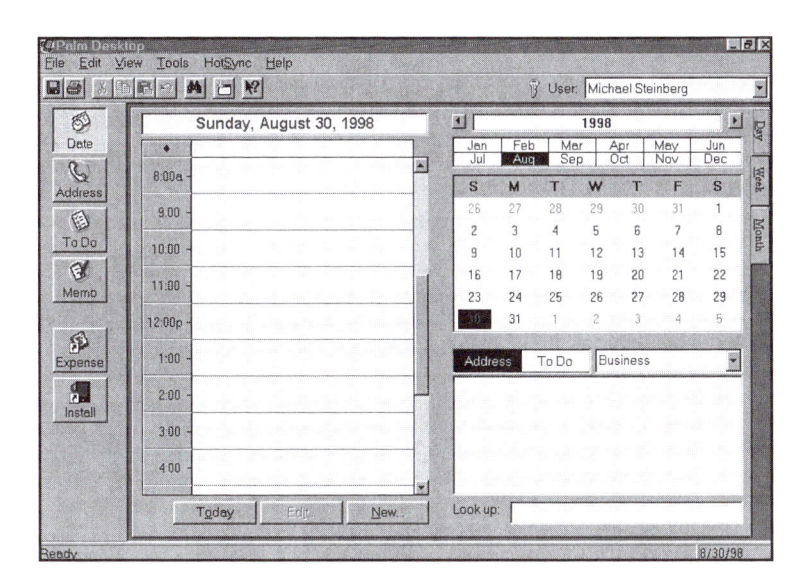

FIGURE 17.2 Main Palm Desktop screen.

2. Click the Date Book button, located on the left side of the screen. This brings up the main Date screen showing today's date in the Day view (see Figure 17.3).

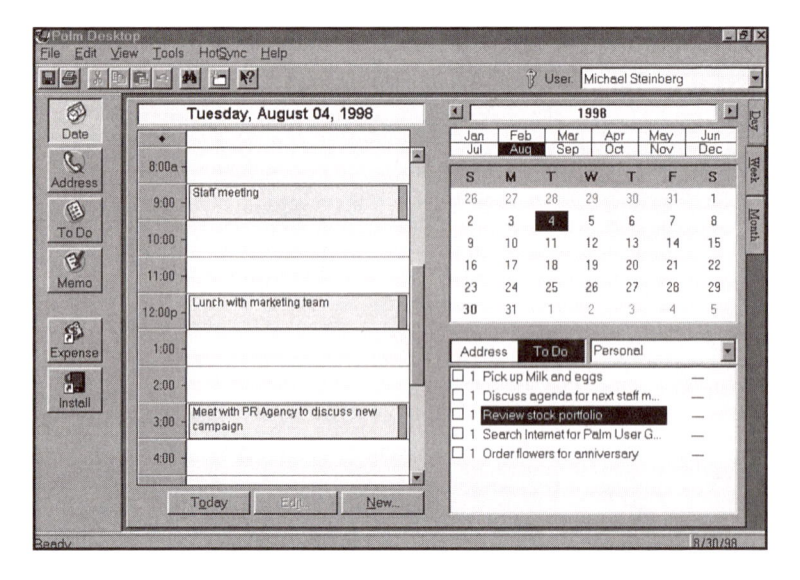

FIGURE 17.3 Main Date screen—Day view.

SELECTING ANOTHER DATE TO VIEW

If you want to look at another date, follow these steps:

1. To select the year, use the left/right arrows located on each side of the year displayed at the side of the screen until the correct year appears.

2. To select the month, tap the correct month from the list that appears below the year indicator.

3. To select the day, tap the correct day from the list displayed below the month list. When you select the day, the application will automatically display the activity for that date.

ADDITIONAL CALENDAR VIEWS

You can switch to a Week (see Figure 17.4) or Month (see Figure 17.5) view by clicking the applicable tab located at the far right of the screen.

DESKTOP APPLICATIONS—DATE BOOK 189

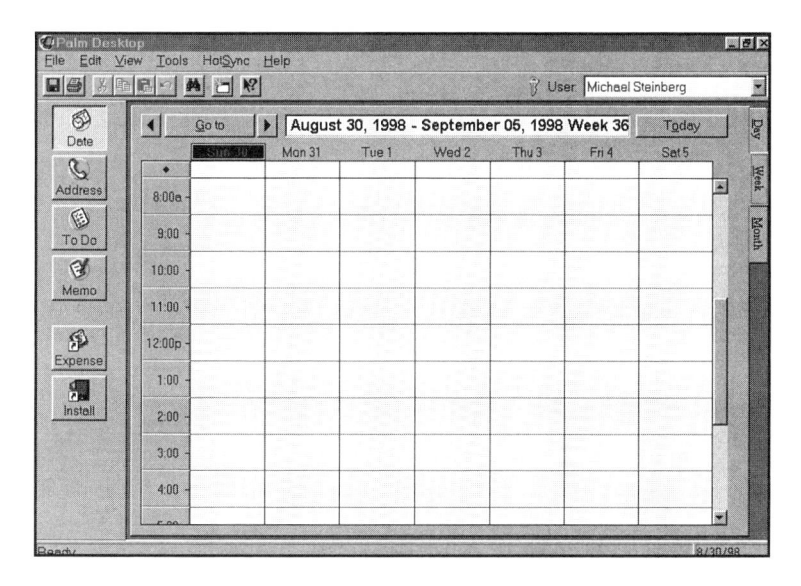

FIGURE 17.4   Main Date Book screen—Week view.

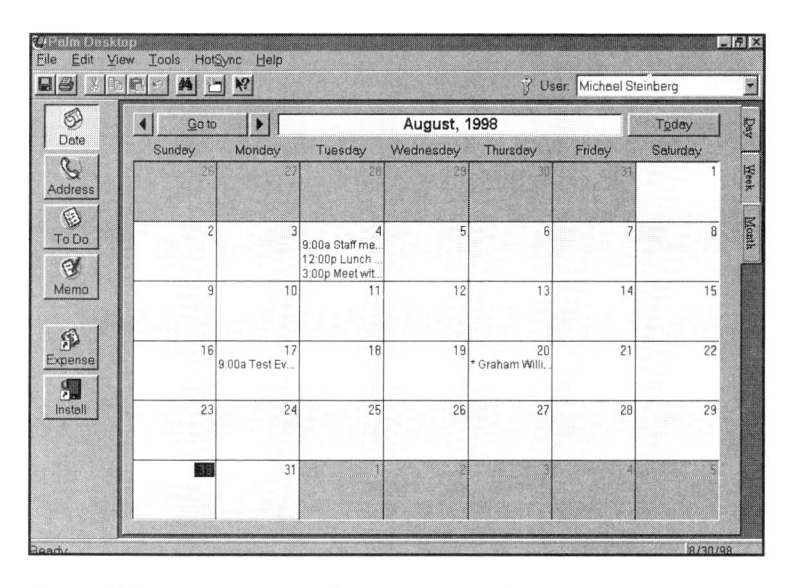

FIGURE 17.5   Main Date Book screen—Month view.

ADDING A NEW ENTRY

You can add a new entry in the following four ways:

- From the keyboard, press Ctrl-N, or

- Click the New button, located in the lower middle of the screen. The Edit Event screen appears (see Figure 17.6), or

- Select Edit, New Event from the pull-down menus located at the upper left of the screen, or

- Click the hour that you wish the event to start directly from the calendar. You can then enter a description of the event (see Figure 17.7).

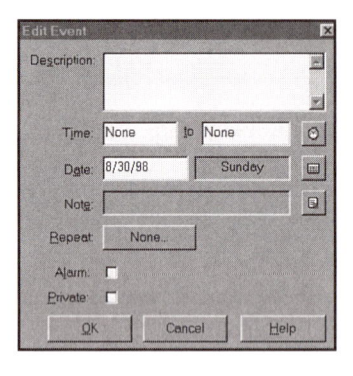

FIGURE 17.6 Edit Event screen.

On the Edit Event screen, you can add specific information about this event:

- Description   Enter a brief description of the event

- Start and end time   You may set or change the start end times here. This may be done manually or by clicking on the clock icon to the right. This will bring up the Select Time screen (see Figure 17.8).

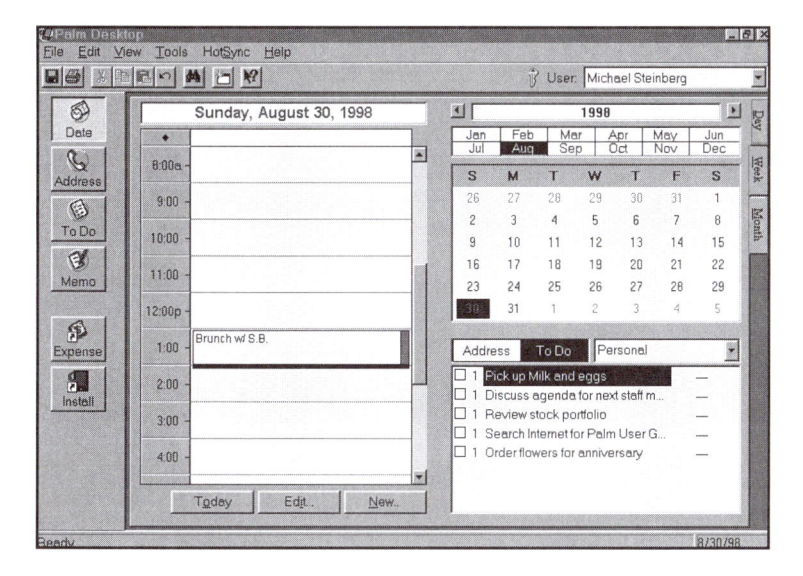

FIGURE 17.7   Main screen—enter description directly.

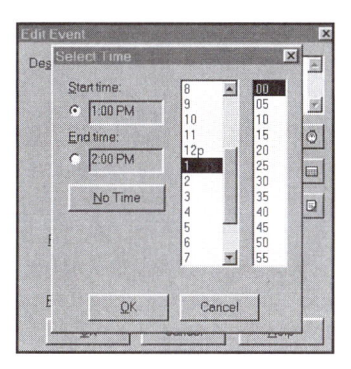

FIGURE 17.8   Select Time screen.

- Date   You can set or change the date here. This can be done manually or by clicking the Calendar icon to the right, which brings up the Select Date screen (see Figure 17.9).

FIGURE 17.9 Select Date screen.

- Note   You can add a note about the event here. This may be done by clicking on the Note field or by clicking the Note icon to the right. This brings up the Note Editor (see Figure 17.10).

FIGURE 17.10 Note Editor.

- Repeat   The default for a new entry is None. If you wish to make this a repeating event, click None. This brings up the Change Repeat screen (see Figure 17.11).

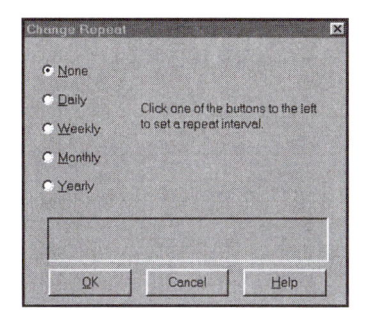

FIGURE 17.11   Change Repeat screen.

As you can see from the Change Repeat screen, you can set the event to repeat daily, weekly, monthly, or yearly. The setting you choose will depend on the type of event. For example:

- Weekly   Perhaps taking out the trash or attending a staff meeting.
- Monthly   Perhaps attending a social event, such as a computer user group meeting.
- Yearly   Perhaps a birthday or anniversary.
- Alarm   You can set an alarm for this event by clicking the box. If you do so, you are asked to tell the system when you want the alarm to occur. You do this by filling in the fields that appear (see Figure 17.12).

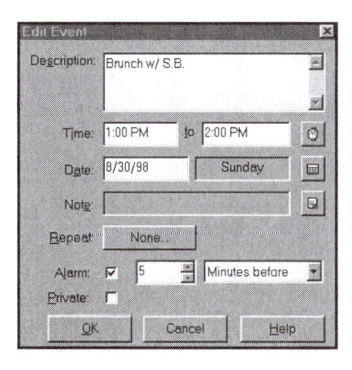

FIGURE 17.12   Set Alarm screen.

- **Private** You can mark the event Private by clicking the check box. If the message is marked Private, you must enter a password to view it.

> **Second Event—Same Time** You can add a second event at the same time period by clicking on the hour of the event. A second description box will appear (see Figure 17.13).

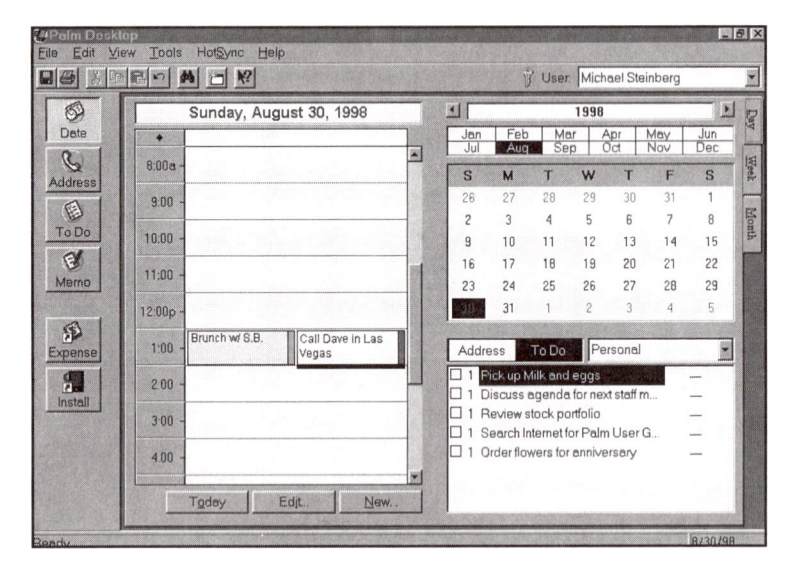

FIGURE 17.13 Date Book screen showing two events occurring at the same time.

VIEW AN EXISTING EVENT

To see an existing event and all the information already in the Date Book, follow these steps:

1. Highlight the event by clicking on it once.
2. Click the Edit button.

    Or…

Click the Edit drop-down menu and click Edit Event.

3. The details are now available on the Edit Event screen (see Figure 17.14).

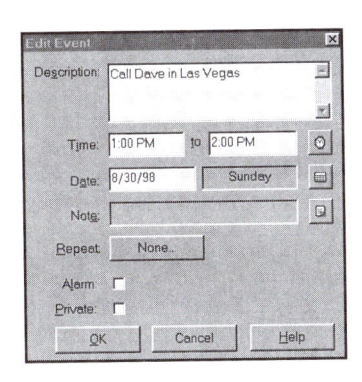

FIGURE 17.14 Edit Event screen.

If there is a note associated with this event, you can view the note's contents by double-clicking the Note icon, located above the event description (See Figure 17.15).

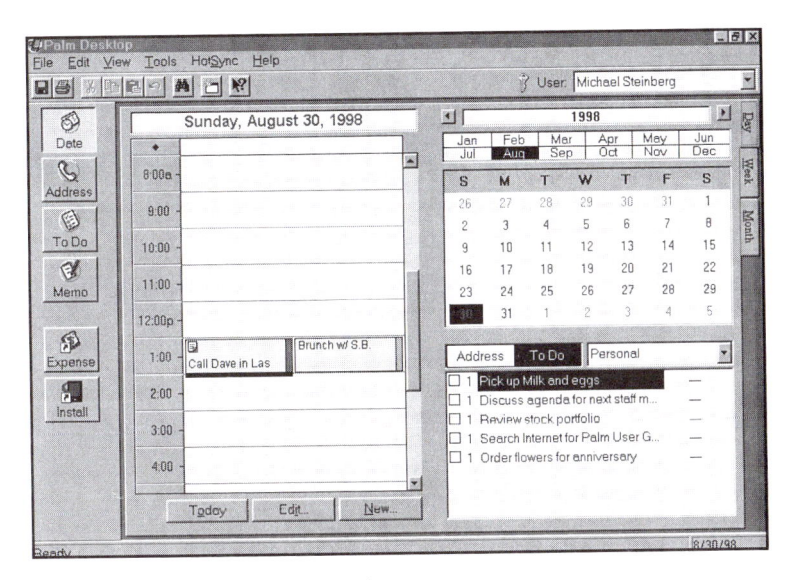

FIGURE 17.15 Date Book Note icon.

Accessing the Address Book and To Do List

The Palm Desktop Address Book program is designed to give you the ability to look at information from the Address Book and To Do List programs from this screen. You can cut and paste data into the Date Book without leaving the program.

Accessing the Address Book

While using the Date Book, you can access data from the Address Book (see Figure 17.16) by following these steps:

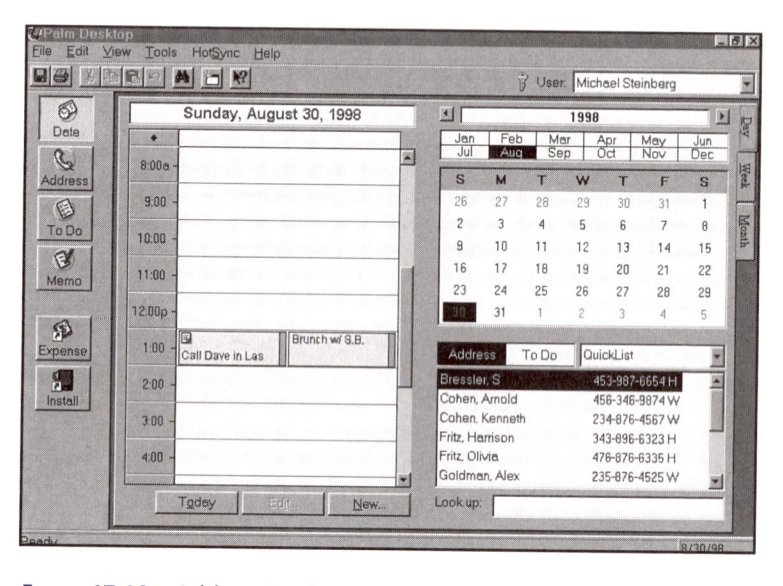

Figure 17.16 Address Book access screen.

1. Click on the word Address located on the lower-right section of the screen.

2. To view the list of names in your Address Book, scroll down the list using the slide or arrows to the right of the list.

3. If you wish to see only a specific category in the Address Book, open the drop-down category list located to the right and click on the category you wish.

4. To find a specific name, enter that name in the Look up field located at the lower-right portion of the screen.

> **Direct Access to the Address Book** To jump directly to the Address Book, double-click on either the word Address or on a specific name from the list. This will take you to the Address Book main screen can (see Figure 17.17).

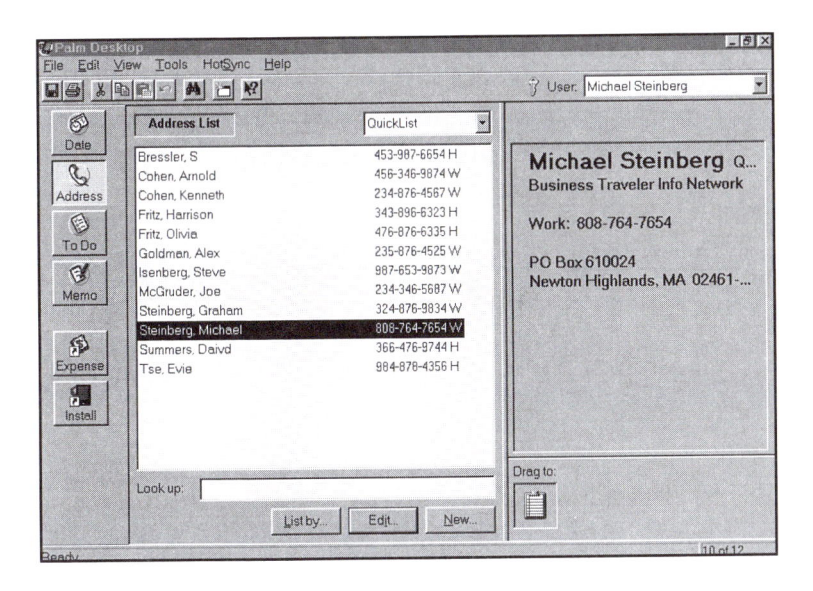

FIGURE 17.17 Address Book main screen.

ACCESSING THE TO DO LISTS

To view your To Do Lists while in the can Address Book program (see Figure 17.18), follow these steps:

198   LESSON 17

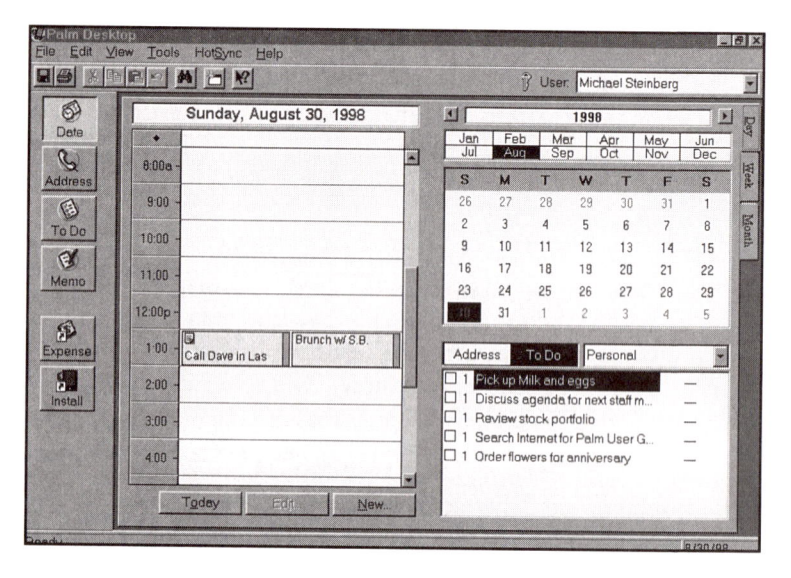

FIGURE 17.18   To Do List access screen.

1. Click on the words To Do.

2. To view To Do List, scroll down the list using the slide or arrows to the right of the list.

3. If you wish to see only a specific category in the To Do List, open the drop-down category list located to the right and click on the category you wish.

> **Direct Access to the To Do List**   To jump directly to the To Do List program, double-click on either the word Address or on a specific name from the list. This will take you to the To Do List main screen (see Figure 17.19).

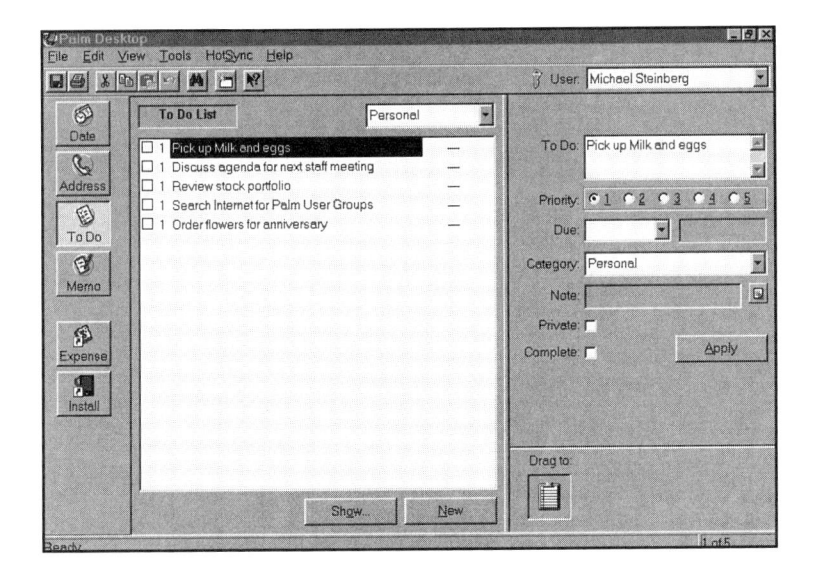

FIGURE 17.19 To Do List main screen.

In this lesson, you learned about the Desktop Date Book. The next lesson covers the Desktop To Do List.

Lesson 18

Desktop Software— To Do List

In this lesson, you learn how to create lists using the Desktop To Do List program.

What Is the To Do List?

The Palm Desktop To Do List is just like its Palm hardware counterpart. The *average* To Do list is a piece of paper containing a list of things you plan to do, people to meet, and places to go. The To Do List program doesn't just eliminate the paper, it takes these lists to the next level.

When you make a change on the Palm Desktop To Do List, that change is updated on the Palm hardware when you do a HotSync. In this way, both are kept current.

Opening the To Do List Program

To open the To Do List, follow these steps:

1. Start the Palm Desktop application from the Windows Start/Run, Start/Programs or by using the Palm Desktop icon (see Figure 18.1) on your Windows desktop. This brings up the main Palm Desktop screen (see Figure 18.2).

FIGURE 18.1   The To Do icon.

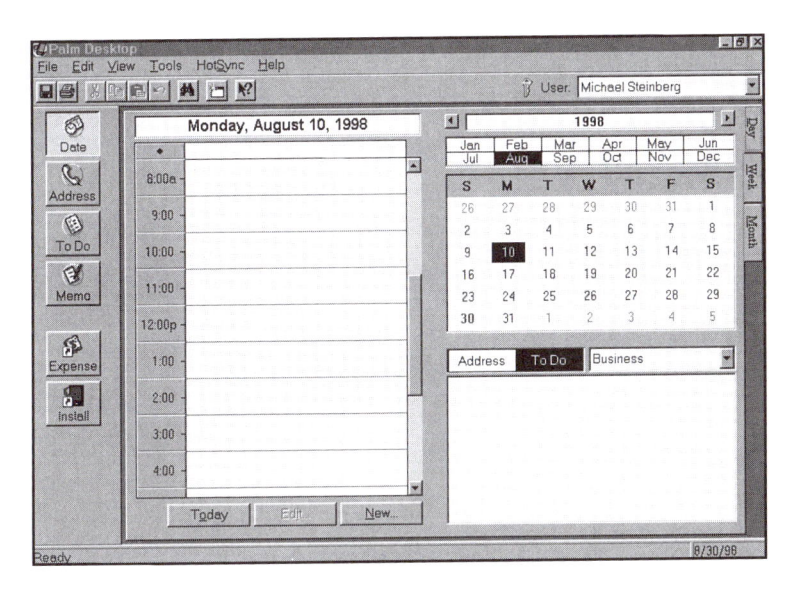

FIGURE 18.2   Main Palm Desktop screen.

2. Click the To Do List button, located on the left side of the screen. This brings up the main To Do List screen (see Figure 18.3).

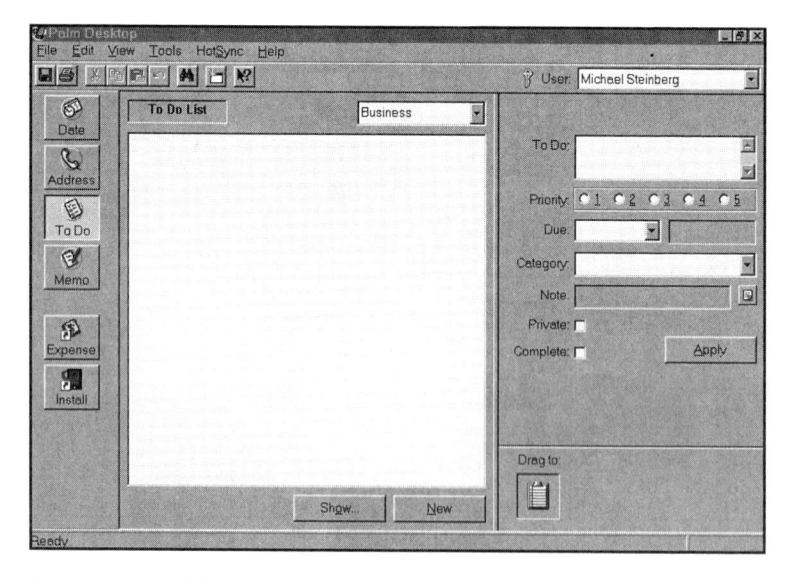

FIGURE 18.3   Main To Do List screen.

ADDING A NEW ENTRY

You can add a new entry in the following three ways:

- From the keyboard, press Ctrl-N, or

- Click the New button located in the lower middle of the screen, or

- Select Edit, New To Do from the pull-down menus located at the upper left of the screen.

Whichever means you choose, a blank field on the To Do List appears (see Figure 18.4). You can then fill in a description of the item.

You can now apply additional details to this To Do List item by using the fields located to the right of the list:

- To Do   Enter a description of the item here.

- Priority   Set the priority level. This determines where the item shows up on the list.

DESKTOP SOFTWARE—TO DO LIST

- **Due** Choose a due date from the list provided. If you want a specific date, click Choose date from the list. This brings up Select Date screen (see Figure 18.5).

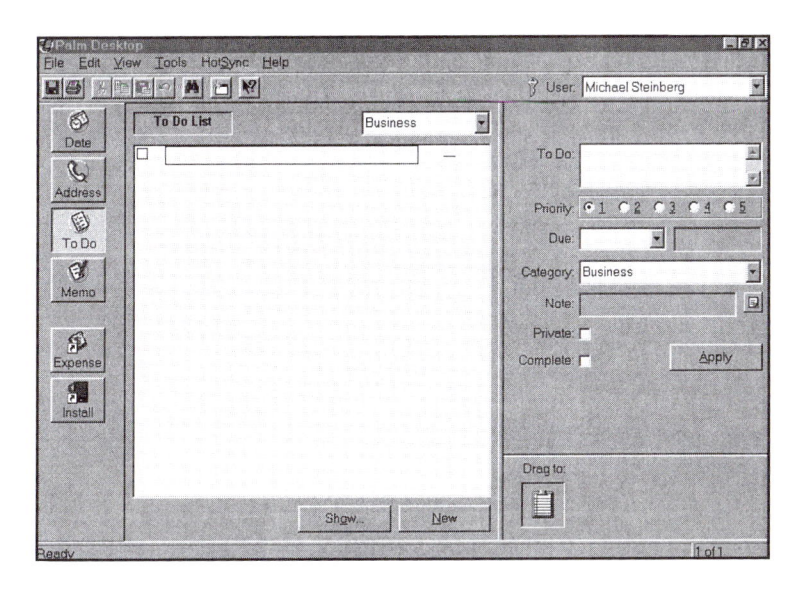

FIGURE 18.4 Blank To Do List item.

FIGURE 18.5 Select Date screen.

- **Category** You can assign this item to a specific category by using the list to the right. If you wish to add a new category, choose Edit Categories. This brings up the Edit To Do Categories screen (see Figure 18.6).

204　LESSON 18

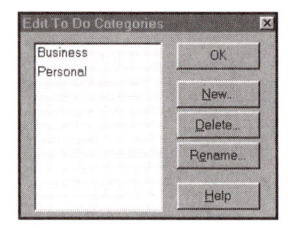

FIGURE 18.6　Edit To Do Categories screen.

> **Categories Can Help**　If you plan to have large amounts of To Do items, consider the use of categories. If you can segment your items into just a few categories, it will make them easier to locate and display.

- Note　You can add a note about the event here. This may be done by clicking on the Note field or by clicking the Note icon to the right. This brings up the Note Editor (see Figure 18.7).

FIGURE 18.7　Note Editor.

- Private　You can mark the event Private by clicking the check box. If the message is marked Private, you must enter a password to view it.

- Complete   You can designate the item as complete or not complete by checking or unchecking the box.

Changing Category Views

If you have elected to assign your To Do list items to multiple categories (as discussed previously in this lesson), you need to know how to view the different categories.

To view a different category, follow these steps:

1. Click the Category pull-down menu located at the upper-middle portion of the screen, above the To Do List.
2. Click the category you wish to view.
3. The new To Do List for that category then appears onscreen.

Show To Do Preferences

You can control how the To Do items are displayed. To set the preferences, click the Show button located at the lower-middle portion of the screen. The Show Options screen appears (see Figure 18.8).

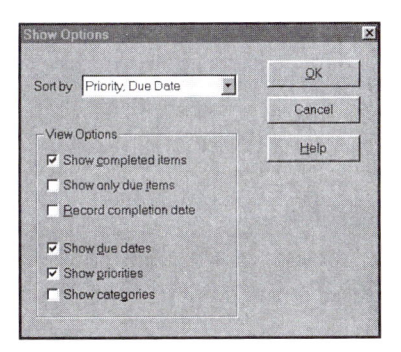

FIGURE 18.8   Show Options screen.

From here, you can set the following parameters:

- Sort by
- View Options:

    Show completed items

    Show only due items

    Record completion date

    Show due dates

    Show priorities

    Show categories

> **Preferred Display** You can pick and choose your preferences here to meet your specific needs. You might only want to see due items to get an overview of what is due now. Then, later, you might want to see due and completed items to see what percent of the work has been completed. You can switch back and forth whenever you want.

In this lesson, you learned how to enter and view To Do List items on the Desktop. The next lesson covers using the Desktop Memo Pad program.

Lesson 19

In this lesson, you learn how to create and view documents using the Palm Desktop Memo Pad software.

Desktop Software—Memo Pad

What Is the Memo Pad?

Like its Palm counterpart, the Memo Pad is a very basic word processor, perfect for jotting down quick notes, instructions, or other useful information.

The Memo Pad can hold all that information that would otherwise take up space in your wallet or briefcase. Many travelers keep their frequent traveler numbers in a Memo Pad entry, for example, instead of carrying around all those cards. You can use it to store driving directions, brief meeting notes, travel itineraries, or ideas for an upcoming project. I used it at a trade show to keep a list of booths I planned to visit, instead of carrying the trade show guide.

As with the other desktop programs, any change made to the Memo program will be updated on the Palm hardware during the HotSync.

> **Time Saver** If you have an extensive amount of Memo data to add, you might be better off entering from the Desktop then using HotSync. From the Desktop, you can enter the data from the keyboard or use Cut and Paste, which can save a considerable amount of time compared to using Graffiti or the Palm soft keyboard.

STARTING THE MEMO PAD PROGRAM

To open the Memo Pad, follow these steps:

1. Start the Palm Desktop application from the Windows Start/Run, Start/Programs or by using the Palm Desktop icon (see Figure 19.1) on your Windows desktop. This brings up the main Palm Desktop screen (see Figure 19.2).

FIGURE 19.1 The Memo icon.

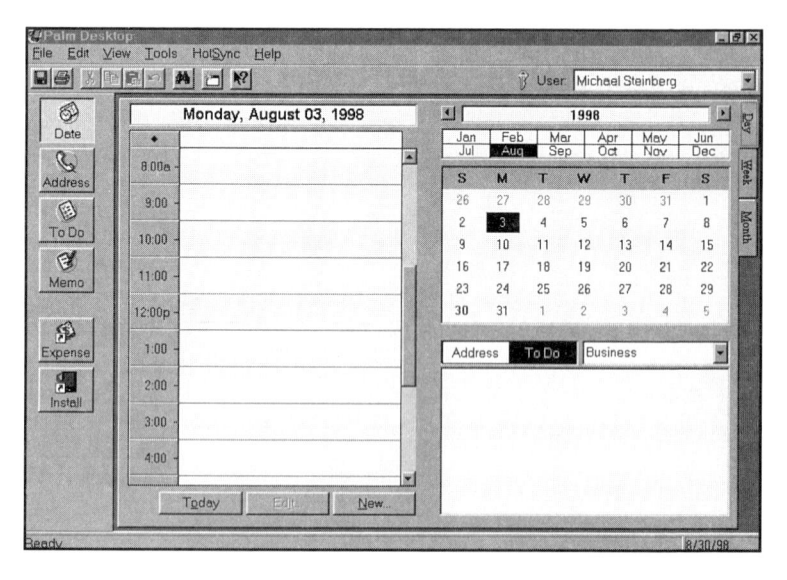

FIGURE 19.2 Main Palm Desktop screen.

2. Click the Memo Pad button, located on the left side of the screen. This brings up the main Memo Pad screen (see Figure 19.3).

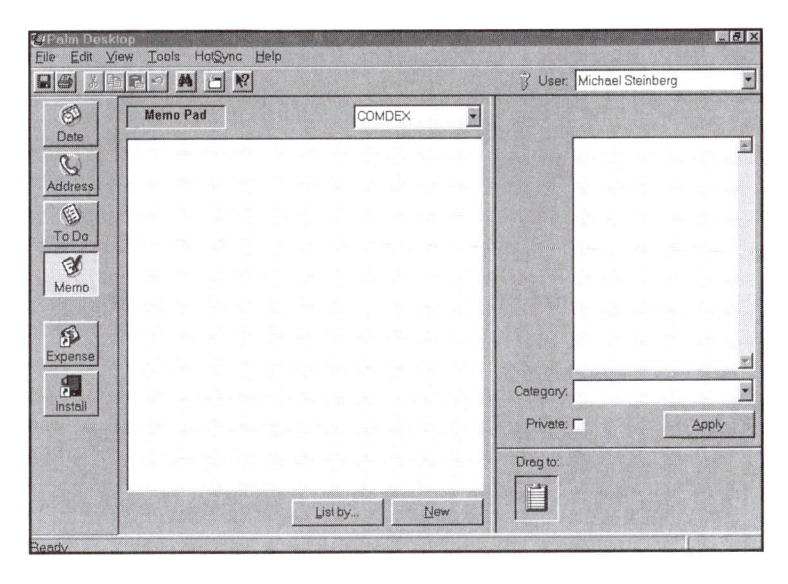

FIGURE 19.3 Main Memo Pad screen.

ADDING A NEW ENTRY

You can add a new entry in three ways:

- From the keyboard, press Ctrl-N, or

- Click the New button, located in the lower middle of the screen, or

- Select Edit, New To Do from the pull-down menus located at the upper left of the screen.

Whichever means you choose, a blank field on the Memo Pad appears (see Fig 19.4). You can then fill in the description of the item.

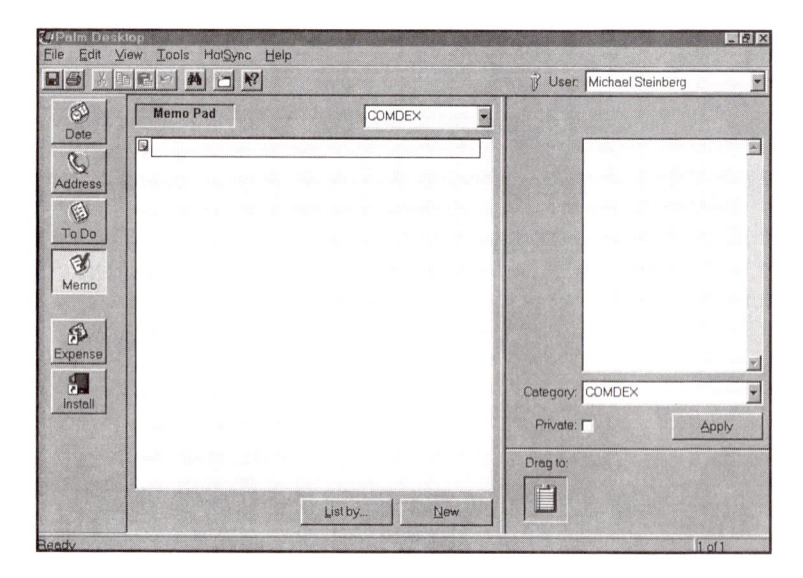

FIGURE 19.4   Blank Memo Pad item.

VIEWING AN EXISTING ENTRY

At the Memo Pad main screen, you have a list of memos available to view. If the list is too long for the display, you can use the up/down arrows or scroll slide to the right to move the list until you locate the file you are looking for. Highlight that file by clicking on it once. The text of the file will appear in the box to the far right of the screen. At this point, you can read or edit the file as you wish.

The list of memos can be displayed either by how they appear on the Palm (based on the last HotSync) or in alphabetical order. To change the appearance, click the List by button at the bottom of the screen. You can then change the order by using the List By screen (see Figure 19.5).

FIGURE 19.5   List By screen.

Changing Memo Details

You can designate the memo as Private or assign a different category at this point as well.

To mark the memo Private, check the box located under the memo text box on the lower-right portion of the screen.

To assign a category, open the category drop-down menu located below the memo text box located at the right side of the screen (see Figure 19.6). Click the new category to assign it. To add a new category, click Edit Categories.

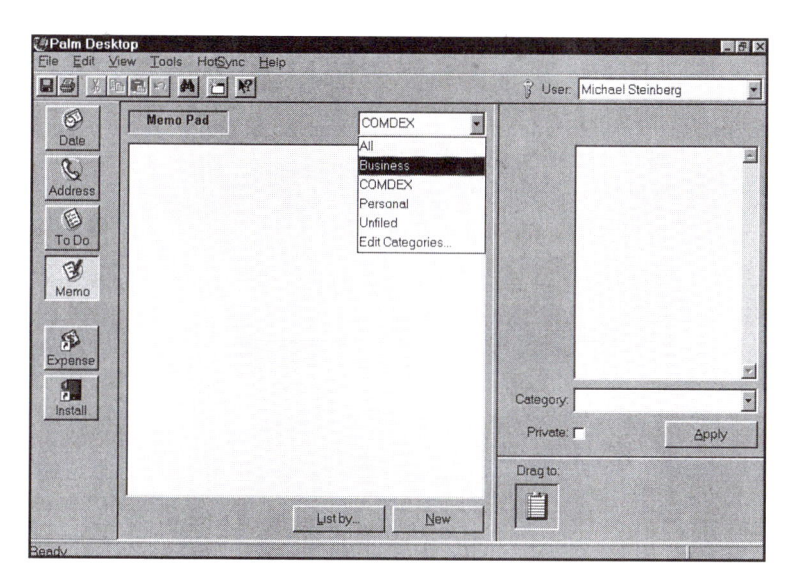

FIGURE 19.6   Category menu.

Deleting a Memo Pad Item

To delete a Memo Pad item, follow these steps:

1. Locate the item you wish to delete.
2. Highlight that item by clicking on it once.
3. Press the Delete key on the keyboard, or

Press Ctrl+D on the keyboard, or

Open the Edit drop-down menu and select Delete.

4. Confirm that you wish to delete this item.

> **Think Before You Delete** As always, be careful when deleting any data. Consider how important it is and whether a backup is available if necessary.

In this lesson, you learned how to add and delete items to the Desktop Memo Pad. The next lesson covers how to use the HotSync program.

Lesson 20
How to HotSync

In this lesson, you learn how to HotSync your Palm with the Desktop software on your PC.

Synchronizing Data with HotSync

Well, we've come a long way. You have:

- Learned about how your Palm hardware works
- Entered addresses, meeting information, To Do List items, and more
- Connected the Palm cradle to your PC
- Installed and used the Palm Desktop software

Now you are about to perform what is probably the most important function of being a Palm owner—HotSyncing.

> HotSync is Palm Computing's name for the act of synchronizing the data in your Palm with your PC, and vice versa. After the HotSync is complete, you have an exact copy of your data on both the PC and the Palm.

You want to HotSync as often as you make changes to either the Palm Desktop programs or the Palm itself. There are two primary reasons to HotSync:

- To keep a backup of your data available. In this way, should the data on the Palm hardware be lost, a quick HotSync will restore it.

- To be sure that you have the most up-to-date information in both places. You want to be sure that you are looking at the latest phone list, schedules, and so on. Otherwise, you might schedule an event where you already have another event planned.

HOTSYNCING FROM YOUR PALM

HotSyncing your Palm and PC is an amazingly easy thing to do. Just follow these steps:

1. Place the Palm in the cradle.

> If it does not fit, don't force it. The Palm should slide into the cradle easily. Don't jam or force the unit into the cradle; this could damage the serial connector.

2. Make sure the HotSync Manager software in running in the background on your PC. It is running if you see the HotSync symbol in the lower-right section of your Windows desktop. If it appears that the HotSync Manager is not running, go to the "Start the HotSync Manager" portion of this lesson.

3. Press the HotSync button located on the lower-right portion of the cradle (see Figure 20.1), or

   Tap the HotSync icon from the Applications main menu (see Figure 20.2).

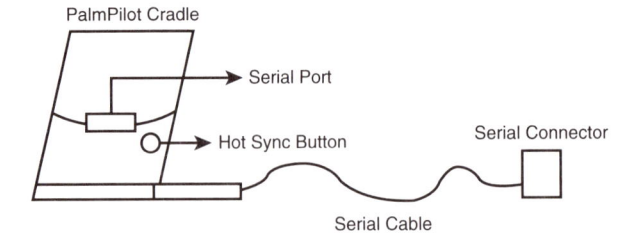

FIGURE 20.1 HotSync button.

How to HotSync 215

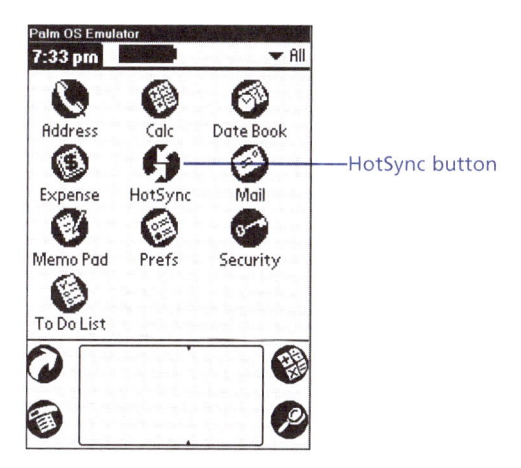

FIGURE 20.2 Main Applications menu.

4. (Palm OS 3.0) The Palm will ask you to identify this as a local or modem-based HotSync (see Figure 20.3).

5. Tap Local. The HotSync program will activate automatically. You will see the status appear on the Palm's screen.

FIGURE 20.3 HotSync screen.

6. (Palm OS 2.0) The HotSync program will activate automatically. You will see the status appear on the Palm's screen.

7. When the sync is complete, you will hear an audible tone and see a message on the Palm.

That's it. That's all there is to it. You are done! See how easy that was?

Starting the HotSync Manager from Your PC

The HotSync Manager is the program that coordinates the HotSync activity between the Palm Desktop and the Palm hardware. It makes sure that all the data is copied so that you have the same information in both places. The program runs in the background in the memory of your PC. Starting the HotSync Manager from the PC is easy. The Palm Desktop software program will automatically install the HotSync Manager so that it will start up when you turn on your PC.

If the HotSync Manager is not running, either

- Double-click the HotSync Manager icon on your desktop (see Figure 20.4).

    Or…

- Use the Windows Start button to locate and run the \Palm\Hotsync.exe program.

Figure 20.4 HotSync Manager icon.

The program will now be running in the background on your system.

SETTING UP THE HOTSYNC MANAGER FROM THE PALM DESKTOP

The Palm Desktop enables you to change certain HotSync Manager parameters, as well as to view the HotSync log. Click on HotSync on the toolbar at the top of the main Desktop screen for the drop-down menu (see Figure 20.5). Let's review each area:

FIGURE 20.5   HotSync toolbar.

- Custom

    This is where you can change the HotSync conduits for each user.

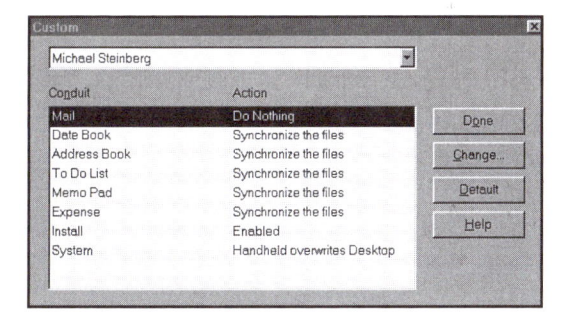

FIGURE 20.6   HotSync Custom screen.

- File Link

    This enables you to link to another file to be used as a source of data such as a corporate database for the company phone list.

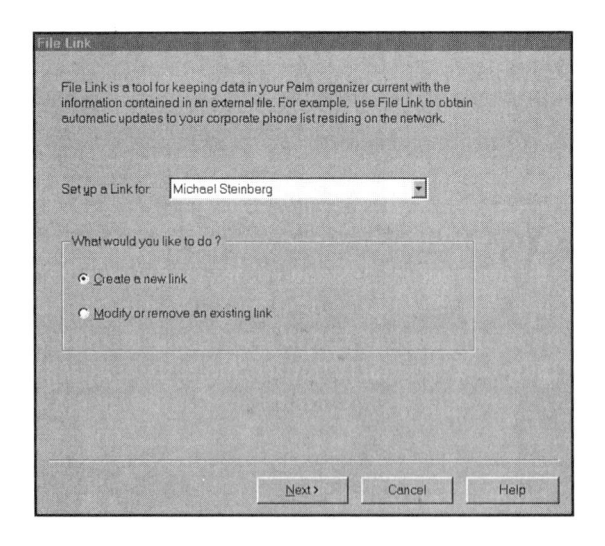

FIGURE 20.7   File Link screen.

- View Log

    You can review the log of your most recent HotSyncs.

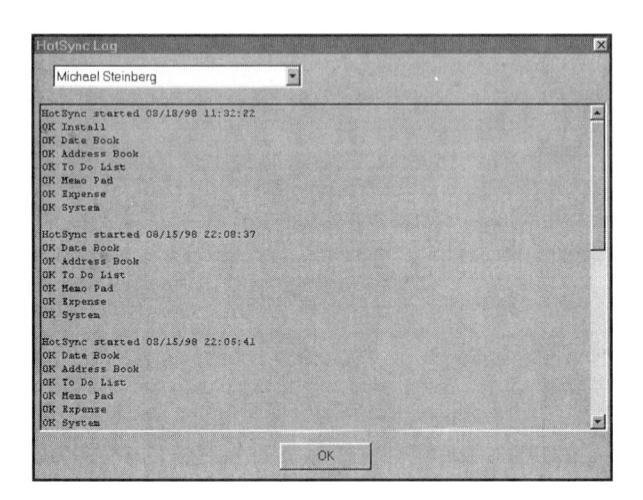

FIGURE 20.8   HotSync Log.

> **Don't HotSync While Viewing the Log!**   The log is updated during each HotSync operation. If you attempt to HotSync while viewing the log, no data will be transferred. In addition, you will not receive an error message.

- Setup

   This is where you set the parameters for the HotSync, including when the HotSync Manager should be installed and what COM port the cradle is connected to.

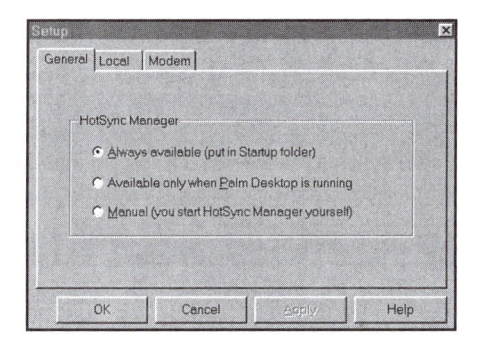

FIGURE 20.9   Main Setup screen.

> **Third-Party Software Support**   A large variety of third-party vendors offer syncing software (called conduits) that enables you to sync your Palm data with their software rather than with the Palm Desktop. If you use another personal information manager, such as Lotus Organizer, check with the vendor to see whether they offer a Palm conduit.

In this lesson, you learned how to HotSync your data between the Palm and your PC. In the next lesson, you will learn how to add new applications to your Palm.

Lesson 21

Adding a New Application to Your Palm

In this lesson, you learn how to add new programs from your PC to the Palm hardware.

Congratulations! You have made it through the basic Palm course. Now it is on to bigger and better things. You are ready to break out. Add new applications. There are so many programs out there to choose from.

Numerous third-party developers have written software for the Palm. You can even write your own programs. I should note that you cannot add just any program. The programs must be written specifically for the Palm.

Adding new software is easy. You can add the following software to your Palm:

- Palm Application Programs (ending with file extension .PRC)
- Palm Organizer Databases (ending with file extension .PDB)
- Palm Organizer Network Config (ending with file extension .PNC)
- Palm Organizer Network Script (ending with file extension .SCP)

You will need to load them onto the Palm to use them. You must first "Install" them, however, using the Palm Install Tool provided with your Palm software—before you HotSync them.

> **Install** This is the act of placing the code of a program in the Palm memory. It is similar to installing software on your PC. In the case of the Palm, the program resides in RAM rather than on a hard drive.

> **RAM** Also known as Random Access Memory, this is where programs and other data are stored on your Palm hardware. Because your Palm does not have a hard drive, all the information must reside in RAM.

Included with your Palm Desktop software is a program called the Palm Install Tool. You should have the icon for this program on your PC desktop.

STARTING THE INSTALL TOOL

To start the Palm Install Tool, do one of the following:

- Click the Palm **Install Tool** icon on your PC desktop (see Figure 21.1).

    Or...

- Use the Windows Start/Run, Palm/Instalapp.exe.

    Or...

- Click the Install button on the main Desktop software screen, located on the lower-left side.

FIGURE 21.1 The Install icon.

This brings up the main Palm Install Tool screen (see Figure 21.2).

222 LESSON 21

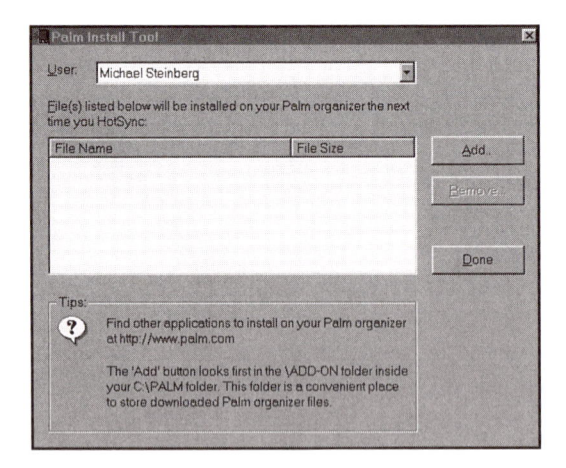

FIGURE 21.2 Main Palm Install Tool screen.

INSTALLING NEW PROGRAMS

You now instruct the program as to which applications to install. To install a new program, follow these steps:

1. Click New.

2. The program will first bring up the **add-on** folder located in the Palm directory (see Figure 21.3).

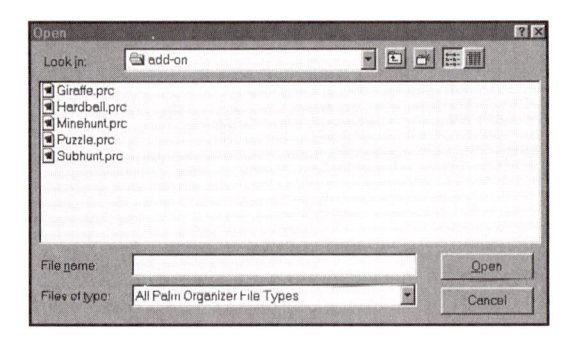

FIGURE 21.3 Open dialog box.

3. If the program you wish to add is shown, click once to highlight it. Then click Add.

4. If the program is not shown, use the Windows Open dialog box to browse your hard drive until you find it. Highlight the program by clicking on it once. Then click Add.

5. Each time you click Add, a program will be added to the Install Tool list. After you have finished adding all the programs, click Done.

6. The Install Tool will prompt you to confirm that all the programs you selected will be installed during the next HotSync (see Figure 21.4).

FIGURE 21.4 Main Palm Install Tool confirmation screen.

7. If you are ready, run the HotSync program as covered in Lesson 20.

> **Will Reload Every Time** After you add a program to this list, it will be installed every time you HotSync until you remove it. This can be an issue if you have intentionally removed a program from the Palm hardware (see Lesson 14, "Memory") to make additional space available.

DELETING PROGRAMS

You can also use the Palm Install Tool to remove programs from the system.

To remove a program from the Palm Install Tool list, follow these steps:

1. Open the Palm Install Tool program. The screen will include the list of software you previously designated be installed.

2. Highlight the program you wish to remove by clicking it once.

3. Then click Remove.
4. You are asked to confirm this action before the program is deleted from the list.

> **Don't Worry** The program is deleted from the list only, not from the hard drive. You can always add the program back at a later time.

> **Where to Find More Programs** As I have said throughout the book, you can find information on other Palm software from your Palm products reseller, Palm user groups, the Internet, or Palm Computing itself. I have included an appendix of Web sites to help you get started. What are you waiting for?

> **Palm Users Group** Palm user groups can be a great source of information. Join your local group today. I have included a list of user groups in an addendum at the end of this book. If you can't find a group in your area, think about starting one!

In this lesson, you learned how to install new programs in your Palm. Go forth and HotSync!

Appendix A

List of Suggested Web Sites

This appendix lists a random sampling of Palm World Wide Web sites.

Hardware

Palm (Palm III and PalmPilot)
> **http://www.palm.com**

IBM (WorkPad)
> **http://www.pc.ibm.com/us/workpad/**

User Groups

Atlanta
> **http://www.avana.net/~mkopack/html/APUG.html**

Boston (New England)
> **http://www.bnug.org/ne-palm or http://www.ne-palm.org**

Canada
> **http://www.kpoole.com/pug/**

Colorado
> **http://www.creativeconsulting.com/coppug.htm**

New York
> **http://www.nypalm.org/**

Philadelphia
> **http://members.wbs.net/homepages/p/h/i/philapug.html**

Stanford
> http://www.rahul.net/flasheridn/spug/

RESELLERS

The Gadgeteer
> http://www.the-gadgeteer.com

I2IUK PalmPilot
> http://www.i2iuk.com

PalmPilot Gear
> http://www.palmpilotgear.com

PDA Central
> http://www.pdacentral.com

INFORMATIONAL

Bookmarks for the PalmPilot
> http://spider.coba.unr.edu/~mccarthy/pmark_show.html

5Business Traveler Info Network
> http://www.business-trip.com

Calvin's PalmPilot FAQ
> http://www.pilotfaq.com

Jay's PalmPilot Web Site
> http://www.creativeconsulting.com/palmpilot.htm

PalmPower Magazine
> http://www.palmpower.com

Pilot.org
> http://www.pilot.org

Ray's PalmPilot Central
> http://www.palmcentral.com

Tap Magazine
> http://www.tapmagazine.com

ZDNet PalmPilot site
> http://www.zdnet.com/products/palmpilotuser/

SOFTWARE (DESKTOP PERSONAL INFORMATION MANAGERS THAT CAN HOTSYNC WITH THE PALM)

Franklin Covey (Ascend)
> http://www.franklinquest.com

Lotus Development (Organizer)
> http://www.lotus.com

INDEX

A

adding
    categories to desktop Address Book, 122, 184
    entries
        Desktop Address Book, 179-182
        Desktop Date Book, 85, 190-194
        Desktop Memo Pad, 209
        Desktop To Do List, 202-205
        expenses, 119
        Memo Pad, 109
    shortcuts to list, 64
    software, 220-224
        application programs, 220
        Organizer databases, 220
        Organizer Network Config, 220
        Organizer Network Script, 220
    see also entering
addition (Calculator), 135
Address Book (Desktop), 68
    categories, 73
        adding, 76-78
        assigning, 74
        editing, 76-78
    desktop, 177
        categories, 183-185
    details, adding, 71
    entries
        adding, 69-71
        finding, 73
        viewing, 72
    menu commands, 78-80
    notes, adding, 72
Address Book icon, 6
address screen, Desktop Address Book, 180-181
adjusting contrast control, 7
alarm
    datebook, setting, 87, 193
    sound, 44
amounts, expenses, 121

applications, 220
    pickers, 19
    starting, 6
Applications icon, 19
assigning categories, Desktop
    Address Book, 183
audio, see sound
auto-off feature, 44

B

backlight display, 7
backups, hotsync procedure, 12
batteries
    changing, 10
    level indicator, 25
beam (infrared), receiving, 45
beam business card, 79
Beam category, 79
buttons
    Cancel, 25
    HotSync, 214
    Menu Soft, 34
    Page Up, 14
    Reset, 13
    setting, 45-49
    soft, 18
        Applications icon, 19
        Calculator icon, 20
        Find icon, 19, 24
        Menu icon, 21
    Startup, 6

C

Calculator, 133
    addition, 135
    division, 136
    functions, 137-138
    menu commands, 138
    multiplication, 136
    opening, 133-135
    recent calculations, 139-140
    subtraction, 135-136
Calculator icon, 20
canceling preferences, 49
categories
    Address Book, 73
        adding, 76-78
        assigning, 74
        editing, 76-78
    changing view, Desktop To Do
        List, 205
    Desktop Address Book, 183-185
    Desktop To Do List, 203
    expenses, 122-124
    Memo Pad
        creating, 111-112
        deleting, 114
        renaming, 113
commands
    Address Book, 78-80
    Date Book
        features, 96-97
        fonts, 94
        preferences, 94-95
    Memo Pad, 115, 138
    menu
        Date Book, 92-93
        edit, 163-164
        expenses, 128-129
        Mail, 147
        main applications screen, 167-168
        security, 159-160
        To Do List, 104-107
    record
        beam business card, 79
        beam category, 79
commas, pauses, 61
connecting hotsync cradle, 172-173

contrast control, adjusting, 7
creating
   categories in Memo Pad,
     111-112
   Mail messages, 144-146
currency
   customizing, 131
   expenses, 126
customizing currency, 131

D

data
   backups, 12
   entering, 27
     Graffiti, 27, 30-31
     onscreen keyboard, 31-33
date, setting, 42, 44
Date Book, 82, 186
   accessing Address Book,
     196-197
   accessing To Do List, 197-198
   adding entries, 85, 190-194
   appointment time, changing,
     87
   date, changing, 87
   features, 86
   menu commands, 92-97
   opening, 82
   repeating events, 88
   setting alarm, 87, 193
   viewing entries, 194-195
     options, 90-91
     specific dates, 83
   weeks to view, 188-189
Date Book icon, 6
dates, format of, 54
defaults

changing, 47
undoing changes, 49
deleting
   applications, 165-167, 223-
     224
   categories
     Desktop Address
       Book, 185
     expenses, 124
     Memo Pad, 114
   Desktop Memo Pad, 211-212
   shortcuts, 66
design, 4-5
Desktop Address Book
   categories, 73
     adding, 76, 78
     assigning, 74
     editing, 76, 78
   desktop, 177
     categories, 183-185
   details, adding, 71
   entries
     adding, 69-71
     finding, 73
     viewing, 72
   menu commands, 78-80
   notes, adding, 72
Desktop Date Book, 82, 186
   accessing Address Book,
     196-197
   accessing To Do List, 197-198
   adding entries, 85, 190-194
   appointment time, changing,
     87
   date, changing, 87
   features, 86
   menu commands, 92-97
   opening, 82
   repeating events, 88
   setting alarm, 87, 193

viewing entries, 194-195
   options, 90-91
   specific dates, 83
   weeks to view, 188-189
Desktop Memo Pad, 207
   adding new entries, 209
   changing details, 211
   deleting, 211-212
   fonts, 116-117
   menu commands, 115
      options, 116
      record, 116
   opening, 108-109, 208
   renaming categories, 113
   view details, 110-111
   view existing entries, 110, 210
Desktop To Do List, 98-99, 200
   adding new entries, 99, 101, 202-205
   categories, 203
   changing category view, 205
   menu commands, 104
      options, 105-107
      record, 104-105
   opening, 200-201
   preferences, 205-206
   viewing details, 101-102
   viewing preferences, 102-103
details
   expenses, viewing, 121-128
   Memo Pad, viewing, 110-111
   networks, 61
dialog boxes
   Edit Address, 182
   Save Draft, 152
   Windows Open, 223
Digitizer, setting preferences, 52
display, 17-18
   backlight, 7
   sharp objects, effect on, 10
division (Calculator), 136

Draft folder (Mail), 152

E

Edit Address dialog box, 182
Edit command, 163-164
editing
   Address Book entries, 76, 78
   categories in Desktop Address Book, 184
   shortcuts, 65-66
electronic Mail, see Mail
email, see Mail
entering data, 27
   characters, 36
   Graffiti, 27, 30-31
   onscreen keyboard, 31-33
   see also adding
expenses, 118
   amounts, 121
   categories, 122
      adding, 119, 122
      deleting, 124
      renaming, 123
   changing date, 120
   currency, 126
   menu commands, 128
      options, 129
      record, 129
   opening, 118-119
   payments, 126
   preferences, 130, 132
   types, 121, 124-125
   vendors, 127
   viewing details, 121-128

INDEX 233

F

Filed folder (Mail), 153
filtering email, 150
Find icon, 19, 24
Find program, 161-162
finding Address Book entries, 73, 182-183
flow control (modems), 57
folders (Mail), 152
    Draft, 152
    Filed, 153
fonts
    Mail, 148
    Memo Pad, 116-117
formats, setting preferences, 53
    date, 54
    numbers, 55
    Preset to (Country), 53
    time, 54
    week starts, 54
functions (Calculator), 137-138

G

game sound, setting, 45
Giraffe
    learning data entry, 30-31
    learning Graffiti, 169-170
Graffiti
    entry pad, 33
    learning
        entering data by hand, 31
        Giraffe, 31, 169-170
    menu soft button, 34
    strokes, 66
    stylus sequence, 35
grocery list, 107

H

hard reset, 12, 15
hardware
    modems
        flow control, 57
        setting preferences, 55-56
        speakers, 57
        speed, 56
        strings, 58
        touchtone versus rotary, 58
        vendors, 56
    PC requirements, 171-172
    setting up, 171
HotSync, 149-151
    backups, 12
    button, 214
    cradle, 172-173
    Manager, 213, 216
        setting up, 217
        starting, 216
    setting preferences, 51-52
    toolbar, 217

I

icons
    Address Book, 6
    Application, 19
    Calculator, 20
    Date Book, 6
    Find, 19, 24
    menu, 21
    To Do List, 6
Install tool
    deleting programs, 223-224
    starting programs, 221-223
installing, 221
    software, 173-176

international characters, 33

J-K

keyboard
    bringing up, 33
        Graffitti entry pad, 33
        Menu Soft button, 34
        Stylus sequence, 35
    changing, 36
    entering data by hand, 31-33
    international characters, 33
    letters, 32
    numbers, 32
    removing, 36

L

letters (keyboard), entering data by hand, 32
lists, 107
locking (security), 159

M

Mail, 141-142
    creating new messages, 144-146
    email signature, 146
    filtering, 150
    folders, 152
        Draft, 152
        Filed, 153
    fonts, 148
    menu commands, 147
        message, 147
        options, 148
    preferences, 148-149
    starting, 142
    truncating, 150-151
    viewing existing entries, 142-144
Main applications
    menu, 215
    menu commands, 167-168
    preferences, 169
main display, 17-18
    backlight, 7
    sharp objects, affect on, 10
manufacturers
    application pickers, 20
    expenses, 127
    modems, 56
    syncing software, 219
Memo commands, Calculator, 138
Memo Pad, 108
    adding new entries, 109, 209
    categories
        creating, 111-112
        deleting, 114
        renaming, 113
    deleting, 211-212
    details
        changing, 211
        viewing, 110-111
    fonts, 116-117
    menu commands, 115
        options, 116
        record, 116
    opening, 108-109, 208
    viewing existing entries, 110, 210
memory, adding to PalmPilot, 16
Memory program (Palm version 2.0), 165
    deleting applications, 165
    starting, 165
Memory program (Palm

INDEX   235

version 3.0), 165
    deleting applications, 166-167
    starting, 166
menu commands
    Edit, 163-164
    Expenses, 128-129
    Mail, 147
        messages, 147
        options, 148
    main applications screen, 167-168
    Memo Pad, 115
        options, 116
        record, 116
    To Do List, 104
        options, 105-107
        record, 104-105
Menu icon, 21
Menu Soft button, 34
Message command (Mail), 147
modems
    flow control, 57
    setting preferences, 55-56
    speakers, 57
    speed, 56
    strings, 58
    touchtone versus rotary, 58
    vendors, 56
multiplication (Calculator), 136

N

Name screen (Desktop Address Book), 179-180
names
    network usernames, 59
    see also renaming
networks, setting preferences, 58
    details, 61
    passwords, 59
    phone numbers, 60-61
    services, 59
    username, 59
Note screen (Desktop Address Book), 181-182
notes, adding to Address Book, 72
numbers
    format, 55
    onscreen keyboard, 32

O

onscreen keyboard
    bringing up, 33
        Graffiti entry pad, 33
        Menu Soft button, 34
        stylus sequence, 35
    changing, 36
    entering data by hand, 31
        international characters, 33
        letters, 32
        numbers, 32
    removing, 36
opening
    Address Book, 177-178
    Calculator, 133-135
    Date Book, 82, 187
    Desktop Memo Pad, 208
    Desktop To Do List, 200-201
    Expense program, 118-119
    Memo Pad, 108-109
    Preferences menu, 39
options commands
    Address Book, 80
    Calculator, 138
    Date Book, 93
        features, 96-97
        fonts, 94
        preferences, 94-95
    expenses, 129
    Mail, 148

main applications screen, 168
Memo Pad, 116
security, 159-160
Organizer databases, 220
Organizer Network Config, 220
Organizer Network Script, 220
owner preferences, 62-63

P

packing list, 107
Page Up button, 14
Palm III (1998) features, 3
PalmPilot
    adding memory, 16
    Address Book, *see* Address Book
    changing batteries, 10
    Date Book, *see* Date Book
    design, 4-5
    preferences
        alarm sound, 44
        auto-off, 44
        game sound, 45
        opening menu, 39
        set date, 42, 44
        set time, 41-42
        setting, 38
        sound, 44
    resetting, 12
        hard reset, 12, 15
        semisoft reset, 12, 14
        soft reset, 12-13
        warm reset, 12, 14
    starting, 1, 5
        power switch, 6
        startup buttons, 6
PalmPilot 1000 (1996), 2
PalmPilot 5000 (1996), 2
PalmPilot Personal, 2
PalmPilot Professional Edition (1997), 2

features, 2
WorkPad, 3
passwords (security)
    assigning, 157
    changing, 158
    forgotten, 159
    networks, 59
pauses, commas, 61
payments, expenses, 126
PC hardware requirements, 171-172
PDA (Personal Digital Assistant), 1-2
pen, setting preferences, 49-50
Personal Digital Assistant (PDA), 1-2
phone numbers, networks, 60-61
power switch, starting PalmPilot, 6
preferences
    alarm sound, 44
    auto-off, 44
    Desktop To Do List, 205-206
    expenses, 130, 132
    game sound, 45
    Mail, 148-149
    Main applications, 169
    opening menu, 39
    set date, 42, 44
    set time, 41-42
    setting, 38
        beam receive, 45
        buttons, 45, 47-48
        canceling settings, 49
        categories, 38
        defaults, 47
        Digitizer, 52
        formats, 53-55
        HotSync, 51-52
        modem, 55-56
        networks, 58-61
        owner, 62-63
        Pen, 49-50
        shortcuts, 63-64

INDEX   237

sound, 44
viewing To Do List, 102-103
Preset To (Country) format, 53
private records (security), 156-157

Q-R

Quick Tour, 176

RAM (Random Access
  Memory), 221
receiving beams (infrared), 45
Record command
    Address Book, 79
    beam business card, 79
    beam category, 79
    Date Book, 92
    Memo Pad, 116
records, private, 156-157
removing
    keyboard, 36
    stylus, 9
renaming
    categories
        *desktop Address Book,
        184*
        expenses, 123
        Memo Pad, 113
    see also names
replacing stylus, 9
reprogramming buttons, 45-49
Reset button, 13
resetting PalmPilot, 12
    hard reset, 12, 15
    semisoft reset, 12, 14
    soft reset, 12-13
    warm reset, 12, 14
    see also setting preferences
rotary lines (modems), 58

S

Save Draft dialog box, 152
searching, Find program, 161
security
    features, 155
    locking, 159
    menu commands, 159-160
    passwords
        assigning, 157
        changing, 158
        forgotten, 159
    private records, 156-157
    starting, 156
semisoft reset, 12, 14
services, network, 59
setting preferences, 38
    auto-off, 44
    beam receive, 45
    buttons, 45, 47-48
    canceling settings, 49
    categories, 38
    date, 42, 44
    defaults, 47
    Digitizer, 52
    formats, 53-55
    game sound, 45
    HotSync, 51-52
    modem, 55-56
    network, 58-61
    owner, 62-63
    Pen, 49-50
    shortcuts, 63-64
    sound alarm, 44
    time, 41-42
setting up
    hardware, 171
    HotSync Manager, 217
sharp objects, affect on display, 10
shortcut preferences, 63-64
shortcuts, 66
    adding to list, 64
    deleting, 66

editing, 65-66
signature, email, 146
soft buttons, 18
    Applications icon, 19
    Calculator icon, 20
    Find icon, 19, 24
    menu icon, 21
soft reset, 12-13
software
    installing, 173-176, 221
    PC to Palm, 220-221, 224
        Application Programs, 220
        Organizer Databases, 220
        Organizer Network Config, 220
        Organizer Network Script, 220
sound
    alarm, 44
    setting, 44
speakers, modems, 57
speed, modems, 56
starting
    applications, 6
    Find program, 161-162
    HotSync Manager, 216
    Install tool, 221
        new programs, 222-223
    Mail, 142
    Memory program
        Palm version 2.0, 165
        Palm version 3.0, 166
    PalmPilot, 1, 5
        power switch, 6
        startup buttons, 6
    security, 156
strings, modems, 58

stylus, 9
    removing, 9
    replacing, 9
    sequence, bringing up keyboard, 35
subtraction (Calculator), 135-136
synchronizing data, 213, 216
syncing, see HotSync

T

third-party vendors, syncing software, 219
time
    format, 54
    setting, 41-42
tips, viewing, 36
To Do List, 98-99, 200
    adding new entries, 99, 101, 202-203, 205
    categories, 203
        changing category view, 205
    details, viewing, 101-102
    opening, 200-201
    preferences, 205-206
    menu commands, 104
        options, 105-107
        record, 104-105
    preferences, viewing, 102-103
To Do List icon, 6
toolbars, HotSync, 217
tools, Install
    adding new programs, 222-223
    deleting programs, 223-224
    starting, 221
touchtone lines (modems), 58
truncating Mail, 150-151
turning on PalmPilot, 1, 5
    power switch, 6
    startup buttons, 6

U

undoing preferences, 49
usernames
    network, 59
    see also names

V

vendors
    application pickers, 20
    expenses, 127
    modems, 56
    syncing software, 219
viewing
    Address Book entries, 72, 182
    dates (Date Book), 83, 188, 194-195
    details
        expenses, 121, 123-128
        Memo Pad, 110-111
        To Do List, 101-102
    Mail entries, 142-144
    Memo Pad entries, 110, 210
    preferences, To Do List, 102-103
    tips, 36
    weeks, Desktop Date Book, 188-189

W-Z

warm reset, 12, 14
week starts format, 54
Windows Open dialog box, 223
WorkPad PalmPilot Professional Edition (1997), 3